Greater Springfield ■

Building
on the
Legacy

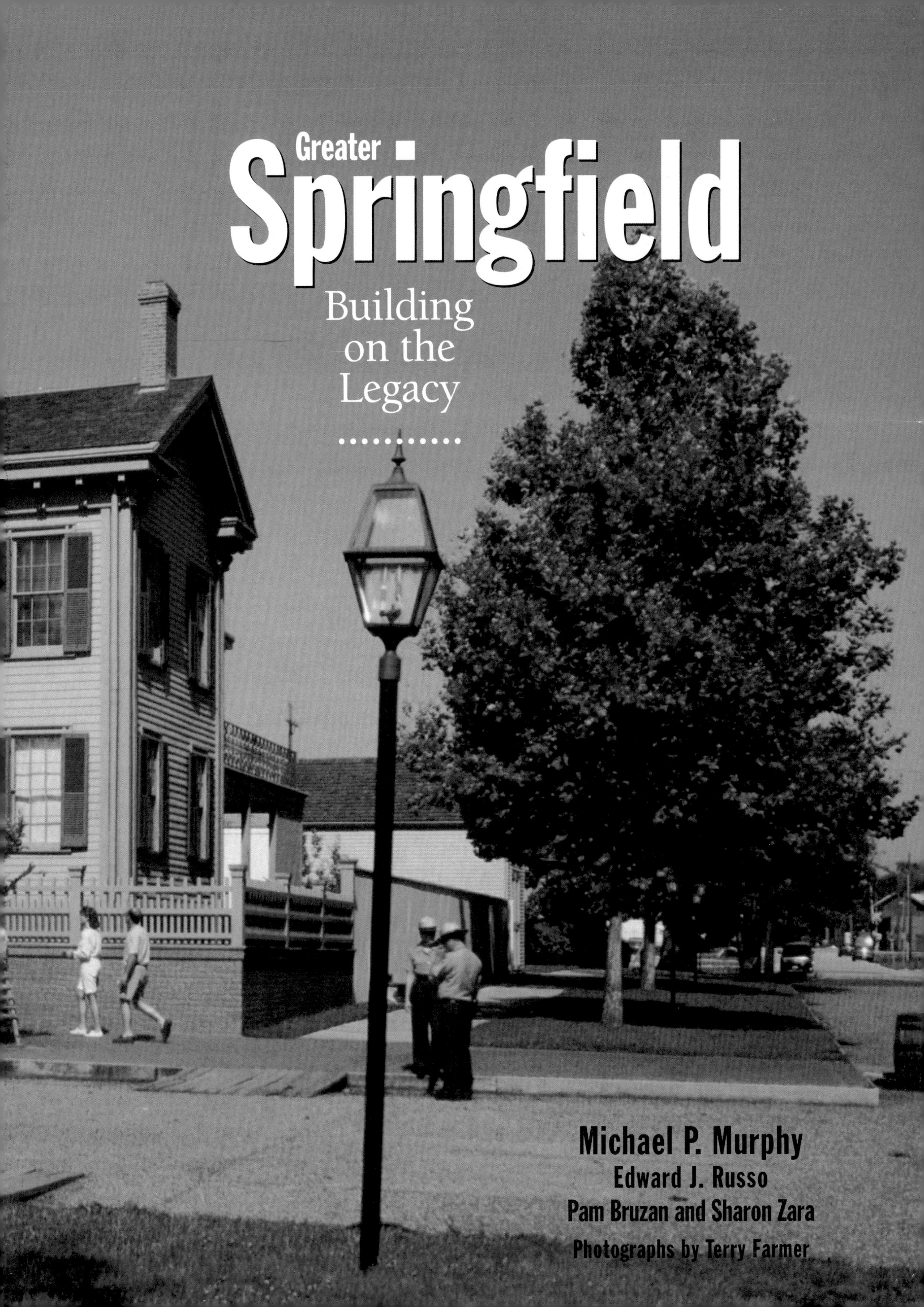

· · · · · · · · · · ·

Michael P. Murphy

Edward J. Russo

Pam Bruzan and Sharon Zara

Photographs by Terry Farmer

Contents

Opposite: Presiding over Springfield's substantial downtown is the silver dome of the Illinois State Capitol.

Right: The Grand Staircase of the Old State Capitol. It was in this building that Abraham Lincoln spoke the immortal words, "A house divided against itself cannot stand...."

FACTORY OF THE ILLINOIS WATCH COMPA

1

River Town Grows Up

S PRINGFIELD, ILLINOIS, IS a town that by all conventional reasoning should not exist—at least not as a prosperous, midsize American city and capital of one of the richest states in the nation.

Anyone in Springfield's first days who had predicted a bright economic future for the ragged little settlement would have been dismissed as a hopeless dreamer. And indeed, Springfield at first seemed to have all the wrong elements for a flourishing city. But those who overlooked the little village ignored the most important resource in the making of a successful city—determined citizens.

Many thousands of years before permanent settlement in the place we now call Springfield, the Sangamon River Valley was shaped by the Illinois Glacier, which leveled hills and filled the valley with tons of pulverized stone and clay. The two substances mixed to form some of the richest agricultural land in

The large and impressive plant of the Illinois Watch Company symbolized the first industrial age in Springfield, in the nineteenth century. Its famous timepieces were particularly prized by railwaymen. The factory stood at Ninth Street and North Grand Avenue.

the world. Enormous veins of coal below the surface of this rich soil had begun forming nearly 300 million years earlier.

Frenchmen coming from Canada in the 1600s were the first Europeans to visit Illinois. Marquette and Joliet were among the later explorers who traveled into central Illinois before it was ceded to the new state of Virginia in 1778 as the County of Illinois. That "county" included present-day Illinois, Ohio, Indiana, Michigan and Wisconsin. Most of this land was perceived as untamed, even "useless," wilderness when the Northwest Ordinance of 1787 opened it to permanent settlement and the first new Americans moved into the region. This trickle of immigrants became a flood, and places like Shawneetown, Illinois, on the Ohio River (Illinois' southern border) became crowded towns. Shawneetown was the main entrance to the territory. And Kaskaskia was the first capital when Illinois entered the Union as the 21st state, in 1818. In 1817, while Illinois was preparing for statehood, Robert Pulliam, a farmer who lived near present-day Alton, went exploring, and wandered into what is now Sangamon County. He was followed or (perhaps preceded) that same year by Henry Funderburk of North Carolina. Only a few months later, another North Carolinian, Elisha Kelly, described in local histories as "an old bachelor," moved to an unsettled area north of Pulliam near

Spring Creek. He and a brother, John, built a cabin. Various Kelly family members soon joined Elisha, and their colony took the name Springfield.

Those earliest Springfield settlers lived in crude log huts and fashioned an existence as hunters while raising a few crops to supplement their diet. They feared much of the local wildlife, and regularly clubbed wolf packs and snakes to death with spades and crowbars. Their primitive lives were made even more miserable by sickness, especially fever and cholera. Still, stories of the rich land, with its seemingly endless resources of animals to slaughter, open spaces to settle and a rich soil to till, were carried back to other places, and more settlers arrived every year. By 1821, the area around Springfield had become so populated with these hunter-squatters that the new state's legislature created Sangamon County—and Kelly's settlement became the temporary (and later permanent) county seat.

The new United States of America witnessed an incredible move by its citizens to destroy the mysterious wilderness of unsettled land and to conquer time and space by building a gargantuan transportation system of canals, road and railroads (a newly developed form of transportation) across the virgin continent. This "internal-improvements mania," as it was later called, inspired people with the notion that every little settlement might become a teeming metropolis of tomorrow, with its citizens growing rich in the bargain. A mania for real estate speculation accompanied that for transportation.

In Springfield, a new type of settler, the promoter and developer, was arriving and displacing earlier residents. This second wave was personified by Elijah Iles, an ambitious Kentuckian and former cattle herder, who arrived in the new county seat in 1821. Iles shippped a load of goods on the Illinois River to Beardstown, then a thriving port, and brought it overland to Springfield, where he opened a store in July of that year.

Sangamon County had not yet been officially surveyed, which meant that all the settlers were merely squatters. Still, the optimistic Iles laid out and named the town's first streets—Jefferson, Washington, Adams and Monroe, intersected by numbered streets, First through Sixth. When the Land Office did open in November 1823, Iles and another town promoter,

In the 1840s, the Gouveia family, emigrants from Portugal grew grapes on 200 acres north of Springfield, adding a Southern European touch to the American prairie.

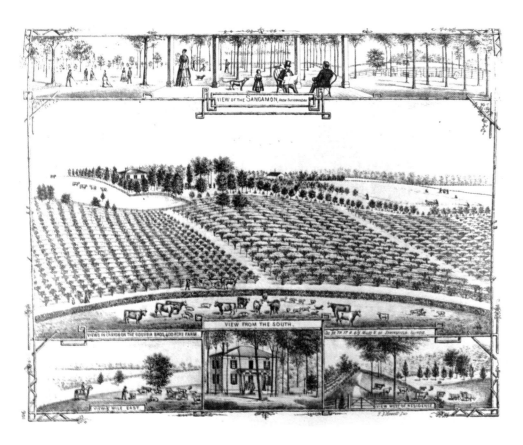

Pascal Enos, together purchased the entire site of Springfield. They changed its name from Springfield to Calhoun (though it would change back again in a few years). They and other hopefuls began to boost and bustle and promote real estate development in the new town, thus beginning a long local tradition of real estate speculation. Iles, Enos and others traded land among themselves almost as often as they sold it to newcomers. Today, the names of Iles and Enos appear on numerous land records, a reminder of those early days of Springfield real estate activity.

Although the state at large was still a raw, sparsely settled area, Illinois was no longer an unexplored wilderness. Settlers were pouring into the southern tip of the state and gradually moving north. Along with the general northward population shift, the state capital was moved from Kaskaskia to Vandalia. The greatly feared "Indian menace" had all but vanished, and one report assured new arrivals that "the murder of a white man by an Indian is now of rare occurrence; more rare than the murder of white men by each other."

Accounts then being written about central Illinois and "Sangamon Country" described the section as one of the most fertile spots in the new West. All manner of people were settling here, and a spirit of tolerance and cooperation was necessary for survival on the prairie. The new immigrant was cautioned that it was well "to throw off and forget many of his former habits and practices and be prepared to accommodate himself to…the circumstances of the country. But if a man begins by affecting superior intelligence and virtue, and catechizing the people for their habits of plainness and simplicity…he may expect to be marked, shunned and called in the way of sarcastic reproach, a Yankee."

In those days, most booming towns were located on navigable waterways and built their wealth on cheap water transportation. New York, Philadelphia, Louisville and, closer to home, Alton, Peoria and even Beardstown and Naples were good examples. Springfield leaders were quick to see that places like Beardstown and Naples were enjoying a prosperous river trade, as numerous steamboats plied the Illinois and Mississippi rivers between these points and St. Louis. In nearby Naples alone, with only 600 permanent residents, more that 300 steamboats arrived and departed annually. Accordingly, Iles and others arranged to bring a steamboat up the nearby Sangamon River. In 1832, the *Talisman* steamed triumphantly along the Sangamon and docked a few miles from town. But even as citizens were rejoicing over the idea of river-town prosperity, the sluggish Sangamon's water level dropped. The *Talisman*

Top: The Civil War tore apart many Springfield families, just as it did throughout America, especially in recently settled areas with migrants from both North and South. Many local people, like these women sewing much-needed bandages, volunteered their time for the war effort.

Bottom: Coal mining was another early pillar of prosperity in the area. Mining is no longer a large local industry, but the old coal shafts still crisscross the earth under downtown Springfield. These miners were photographed in May of 1892.

had to back down river while carefully avoiding stumps and other hazards. The boat caught fire when it reached St. Louis, unhappy investors were left without their money and Springfield seemed left with a greatly diminished future. If it were even to survive, the town must improve connections with the outside world. Communication and transportation improvements were crucial.

While investors pondered how to secure these good connections, the town continued a steady, if undramatic growth; it was officially incorporated on April 2, 1832. By then, northern Illinois was being settled by people from New York and New England, while those from Kentucky, Tennessee, North Carolina and Virginia filled the southern half of the state. These two cultures met, and often clashed, in central Illinois in places like Springfield, which was at the state's midpoint. An 1881 history of Sangamon County records that the Southerners thought Yankees "a tricky, trafficking race of peddlers from New England," while the Yankees dismissed the Southerner as "a long, lank, lazy, ignorant animal…with a large family of idle, hungry, ill-clothed, untaught children." But Yankees and Southerners put aside their differences to build a future for Springfield by financing a successful venture that would assure Springfield an important place in Illinois' future: They made their town the state's capital.

A movement had already arisen to move the state capital, then at Vandalia, further north. Springfield citizens rallied to the fight, offering land and money for a new capitol building and personally pledging for the costs of the move and related expenses. Elijah Iles built a comparatively lavish hotel, the American House, to tempt legislators and their guests. Influential politicians maneuvered on behalf of Springfield's cause and were successful in getting the capital moved in 1837. Plans were quickly drawn for a monumental new Greek Revival capitol by a part-time architect in the town, John Rague. A major financial panic rocked the country that year and nearly brought state government to collapse, heavily burdened as it was by debt related to the internal improvement projects.

In the midst of these dark economic times, Springfield citizens proved their ability to weather adversity and find opportunity in failure. It is a story told and retold by later generations down to the present. Rather than give up in defeat, locals reached into their private savings and personally paid the $16,000 for the state government's relocation costs. At the same time they began proceedings to reincorporate the town as a city and also to develop a reliable, inexpensive transportation system.

As early as 1837, track for the state's new Northern Cross Railroad was being laid near the Illinois River and was aimed at Springfield. By 1842 the first engine reached the young capital. The new railroad, however, was plagued by continued bankruptcies, and worse. Faulty tracklaying was responsible for trains derailing and the occasional iron rail shooting up into the train cars. But Springfield entrepreneurs persevered, and by 1850 had good rail connections with the rest of the country. And the coming of a permanent telegraph operation, in the 1840s, made the latest world news almost instantly available.

It was in the 1840s, too, that state politics added a new and lively dimension to Springfield life. Numbers of lawyers arrived to practice in the courts (including Abraham Lincoln, who had come in 1837) and a whole range of official and semiofficial agencies were founded which, with their attendant officials, employees and budgets, improved Springfield's economic picture. But it was for a brilliant society life that

Summertime plus watermelon equals happy boys. Update the clothes a bit, and add to the ethnic diversity of the children, and this turn-of-the-century picture could be taken in Springfield today.

the city became noted. Balls, levees and soirees were popular diversions among the political crowd, and many newspaper reporters waxed poetic over the silks, satins and low-cut gowns of the ladies. Unmarried daughters were sent by the dozen to board with Springfield relations during the legislative "season." Springfield was on the first step of its climb to being a place of great wealth.

Springfield would become a fully urbanized town during the 1850s and one which had to cope with all of the ills of rapid growth typical in a boom-town economy. A visitor to Springfield in 1850 would have witnessed an astounding amount of physical activity. One could almost feel the expansion in the air. The phenomenal population increase was by itself a sure sign of an aggressively enlarging city. By 1840, 2,600 people were residing in Springfield. That number rose to 3,900 by 1848, to 5,100 by 1850, and to 7,250 by 1855. At the decade's end, over 9,000 residents called Springfield home. The trinity of commerce, railroads and agriculture was responsible for the prosperity visible everywhere. Over 400,000 bushels of wheat and 90,000 bushels of corn were shipped on Springfield railroad lines annually. Retail trade "on a fair Saturday" amounted to $15,000, according to the historian Paul Angle, Every year six million bricks were produced locally and 75,000 pounds of wool were consumed by Springfield manufacturers. The city spread out in all directions. "Construction," says Angle, "was in full swing, and as always when that is the case, the town hummed with activity."

Unfortunately, the place also presented the rough, unkempt appearance characteristic of all boom towns. One Rockford, Illinois, newspaper editor found Springfield to have "neither a pleasant nor cheerful appearance." In fact, he wrote: "There does not appear to be much taste or neatness in the arrangement of things, either of a private or public character.... As to city improvements, it is horrible to think of them. Just think of a city containing seven or eight thousand inhabitants… without a single good sidewalk in it or even a public lamp to light a street."

Sadly, these observations were only too true. And in addition to the ugliness, the squalor of wandering pigs, horse droppings and rotting garbage in the streets contributed to poor public health conditions. Most citizens, however, were more concerned with moneymaking than in prettying up a town. With the steady transition from a barter economy to one relying on cash and credit, more banking services were needed. It was in the 1850s that Springfield's (and Illinois') oldest bank, Bank One, was founded.

Still, rhetoric like the Rockford editor's notwithstanding, citizens did make progress. The public school system, police department, public water supply and first fire department were all in existence by the 1850s. Springfield even grew large enough to merit its first full city directory, published in 1855. Grand mansions were going up, especially in the neighborhood which came to be known as Aristocracy Hill, around the Illinois Governor's Mansion. By 1860,

Above: The old Romanesque Revival City Hall stood proudly from 1892 until 1961, when it was replaced by the Municipal Building, head-quarters of the city's government today.

Left: For two years, from 1908 to 1910, Rayfield and Springfield automobiles were manufactured in Springfield. A distinctive feature of the cars—engines painted a light cream color and adorned with polished brass fittings—won over many buyers.

on the eve of the American Civil War and the year Abraham Lincoln was elected president of the United States, his hometown was eagerly looking to continued growth and prosperity.

The Civil War had a very direct social effect on Springfield. Because the place had been settled by so many Southerners, there was great anguish on

Top: Government employment—federal, state, county and city—has always been an important part of Springfield's economy. These workers for the Internal Revenue Service, seen here in about 1915, have the same no-nonsense look that one imagines their IRS successors have today.

Bottom: The 1920s saw a golden age of baseball in Springfield. This stock certificate represents part of the $50,000 raised from fans to build the stadium, Lanphier Park, which is still enjoyed today.

the part of those who had relations fighting on both sides of the conflict. In some cases brother fought against brother. The city did benefit financially from government contracts and a consequent influx of money. Springfield took on the aspect of an industrial city, with increased railroad traffic and stepped-up manufacturing and production. By 1865, for example, more cattle were being fed for slaughter in Sangamon County than anywhere else in the state.

In the years immediately following the Civil War, Springfield mirrored the national optimism about a brighter tomorrow in a rapidly industrializing world. The last stagecoach line had closed in 1860, making railroads the primary form of cheap, efficient and modern travel. The rich agricultural bounty from the surrounding county was shipped out and the latest news, fashions and manufactured items arrived by return freight.

The city spread out in every direction. By 1870, the fast-growing outlying districts were connected with downtown by a streetcar system, which had been inaugurated in 1861. The population had almost doubled since the outbreak of the Civil War and 1870 found Springfield with 17,364 inhabitants. Encouragement by a newly founded Board of Trade (ancestor of the Greater Springfield Chamber of Commerce) resulted in the establishment of the three foundries, a boiler works, two carriage manufacturers, implement works, numerous smaller businesses and the Illinois Watch Company.

Local industries were powered with steam generated by another Springfield resource, coal. From the opening of the first mine, at the end of the Civil War, until the early 1950s, many hundreds of thousands of tons of coal were mined in the immediate area and under much of the present city. Abandoned coal shafts remain under a large part of Springfield today.

The newly urbanized city needed new symbols for its success. An appropriate one was a grand new capitol, which took over 20 years to build after construction began in 1868. The building is still in use as Illinois' capitol and remains the great symbol of state government. For entertainment, local residents could take advantage of traveling theatricals at Rudolph's (later Chatterton's) Opera House, public dance halls, circuses, department store shopping, Wild West shows, large organized picnics, debating societies, a roller skating rink, ladies' groups, clubs and saloons—the last being present in great numbers from the late nineteenth century on. But Springfield was still a place largely in the mud. In rainy weather, elegant carriages, ladies' skirts, children, animals, laborers, aldermen and visitors alike were often splattered with it. The first serious paving program came in the 1870s, as did an elaborate new city water system with a giant reservoir. New city gas and electric plants opened, and by the 1890s, even a telephone company had appeared.

Railroads, mining and industry brought great numbers of laborers to the city, and their settlements added ethnic diversity to neighborhoods. So settled, in fact, was the town that an Old Settlers Society was organized to promote the gathering of county history. Area farmland values doubled—from $50 an acre in 1860 to over $100 by 1870. Land was considered one of the most secure investments and was readily accepted by bankers as collateral. A spirit of optimism prevailed and local editorials lauded the future promise of Springfield. Thus were citizens totally unprepared for the major financial disaster of 1873, which rocked the nation's economy. The infamous Panic of '73 was responsible for so many business failures that its memory was only eclipsed by the Great Depression of the 1930s.

Civic betterment was an idea much used in the local press and pulpits of the day, but seldom put into practice. Taxes to support services were impossibly low, and what was written of as the "lavish spending and outright thievery by numerous city officials" left the city bankrupt at the same time as great private fortunes were being made from the growing industrialization.

The late nineteenth century was a time when Springfield's recognizable neighborhoods were developing. Hundreds of Irish, German and American workers' cottages filled the blocks east of the 10th Street tracks, a fast-developing industrial corridor. The old and the newly rich lived in grand houses on Aristocracy Hill around the Governor's Mansion; and successful second-generation German and Irish lived in substantial comfortable houses on Springfield's North End, which also contained a significant number of Portuguese and the Irish/German "Goosetown" area near Reisch's Brewery. Several dozen new middle-class houses appeared every season on the South Side and West Side, made accessible by the web of streetcar lines from downtown.

By 1900, Springfield was a town of more than 34,000 people, with 200 miles of mostly unpaved streets and a recently electrified streetcar system. The city also boasted 320 manufacturing establishments, five banks, 10 private schools, 46 churches, three hospitals, two orphanages, the Illinois State Fairgrounds, a new City Hall and a public park system. But it also had a statewide reputation for gambling, vice, prostitution and other unlovely businesses. Political corruption flourished in this setting.

But sentiment for political and social reform also gained strength in the early years of the twentieth century. A bloody race riot in 1908, in which two residents were murdered and more than 100 injured, caused Springfield to be vilified across the country for such violence against black people "in Abraham Lincoln's hometown." But the riot also produced one of many sparks needed to ignite the smoldering reform movement. A visit by the evangelist Billy Sunday in 1909 turned more attention on the town. Another, less-well-known temperance minister, William Lloyd Clark, put his impressions of the town into print in a book modestly titled *Hell at Midnight in Springfield, Illinois*. He described a town willing to tolerate all forms of lawlessness. He wrote: "Northeast from the corner of Sixth and Washington streets for many blocks the city is a mass of dive saloons, pawnshops, questionable hotels, fourth-rate lodging houses and brothels, from the lowest ramshackle hovels to the most elaborately equipped which can be found anywhere in the state."

Community leaders and citizens, having suffered enough criticism, mounted a successful political campaign to oust the alderman form of government and replaced it in 1911 with a more "businesslike" commission form. Reform forces in City Hall were buoyed by their victory and launched many needed projects for the city's improvement. Springfield's water supply was now properly treated to reduce disease, the tiny public health department greatly expanded. Careful accounting procedures replaced haphazard ones. An earnest young businessman, Willis Spaulding, was appointed the city's superintendent of the waterworks. Spaulding sold a very lucrative business so that there would be no question of a

> In the prevailing mood of optimism and economic prosperity, the City Council officially adopted a grand city plan.

conflict of interest and went to work for the city making about a third of his former salary. For over 25 years he was in charge of city utilities and made them a nationwide model of efficiency and reliability. Political, business, social, religious and other leaders succeeded in reforming much of the community's once-wayward morals.

The respected Russell Sage Foundation was persuaded to conduct a social survey and to suggest further improvements. The burst of enthusiasm even led to the closing of all saloons in 1917, when Springfield voted itself dry—two years before national Prohibition. That same year the city was crippled by a summer-long streetcar workers' strike indicative of labor's struggle to organize. That cause was centered in the coal industry, and it was around this time that the powerful United Mine Workers President John L. Lewis moved to Springfield. The city remained his official residence during the years in which he was building his U.M.W. empire to the point where it was secure enough to challenge presidential power.

The tragedy of World War I slowed reformers only slightly. After postwar readjustment and the reappearance of prosperity in the 1920s, community leaders again turned their attention to civic improvements. A major street-paving program reached outward to every neighborhood. Tourism increased greatly, as people traveled in their own automobiles to visit Abraham Lincoln's Springfield home via the new "hard roads" connecting Springfield with the rest of the country. A radio station opened, airmail became a regular service and the city's half-dozen movie houses were eclipsed by the grand Orpheum Theater, a million-dollar palace of terra-cotta, plaster and gilding at Fifth and Jefferson streets. Even a 15-story "skyscraper" was constructed on the Public Square by the Central Illinois Public Service Company. In the prevailing mood of optimism and economic prosperity, the City Council officially adopted a grand city plan which called for a major

rebuilding of much of Springfield, a green belt, improved transportation hubs and a new lake. A junior college opened in 1929 as did Pillsbury Mills Springfield plant. Also in the 1920s, the American Business Men's Club, Catholic Charities, Associated Welfare Agencies and Douglas Community Center were formed and joined the already numerous roster of city social, cultural, civic and entertainment groups. In fact, their sheer number caused the *Saturday Evening Post* writer Elise Morrow to quip that Springfield was a "prodigiously organized community."

Nightlife was never livelier. Downtown was a magnet not only for business and shopping but

also for entertainment, theater and illicit drinking at numerous speakeasies. Like many Americans, most Springfieldians in the late 1920s believed that bad times were behind and that more prosperity lay ahead. And, like those in the rest of the country, they were totally unprepared for the catastrophic economic collapse of the Great Depression of the 1930s. The first shock waves of the 1929 stock market crash seemed to leave the town untouched. But as nationwide unemployment rose and farm prices plummeted, the Depression became real. New construction halted. An emergency city Unemployment Bureau tried to serve an average of 850 families a month from a tiny City Hall office;

local soup kitchen volunteers regularly witnessed lines of people two or three blocks long. Springfield's Ridgely Bank closed its doors. And compounding matters, local coal veins grew thinner and thinner and produced less and less. Sangamon County, once the second-highest coal producer in the state, dropped to fourth place by 1930 and ninth by 1940. Hard times had come again.

Springfield, though, was still spiritual heir to the pragmatic do-something civic boosterism which had dealt with earlier social and economic fiascoes like the failure of the steamboat plan and the 1908 race riot. A group of businessmen, bankers, politicians and others emerged with a well-planned attack on the problem. Special scrip was printed to be used in place of money, and a young confident real estate broker, John W. "Buddy" Kapp, came forth as the choice for mayor in 1931. Kapp went immediately to work on economic recovery programs and pushed forward construction of the new lake which voters had already approved in 1930. He obtained federal money for several projects designed to put people to work. Kapp's administration proved so popular that he was elected to four consecutive terms—more than any mayor before or since.

By the late 1930s, construction and employment growth returned. Springfield Hospital announced a complete rebuilding plan. A second public high school, Lanphier, was built on the North Side of town. The Pillsbury and Allis-Chalmers plants each made million-dollar additions. A large public housing project began, the state's Capitol Complex added two major buildings, and private houses and offices were again going up in large numbers. Buses, which had been operating locally since the 1920s, became the only form of public transportation when the streetcars were retired in 1937. Kapp's administration of the 1930s and early 1940s ignored certain negatives, like reappearance of blatant vice, gambling and

Capitol Avenue is one of the most-often photographed streets in Springfield, dominated as it is by the Illinois State Capitol. This view from the late 1930s clearly shows the old Leland Hotel, on the corner at right. Like many of downtown's grand hotels, the Leland has found a new life as an office building.

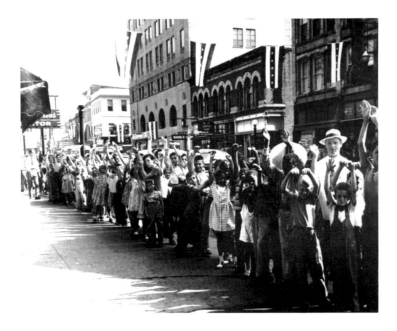

was in short supply and the streets were crowded at all hours of the day and night as many factories worked around the clock to fill government orders. With wartime rationing, Springfieldians shopped carefully for everything from groceries to tires.

By war's end, the city seemed to have grown old and physically shabby from the effects of the Depression and later materials shortages. Its public virtues, too, seemed to have sunk to a low ebb. Gambling and attendant vices once more became so pervasive that investigative reporting by the *St. Louis Post-Dispatch* and an article in the *Saturday Evening Post* again put the city in an embarrassing light before outsiders. And once again, Springfield's people, after an initial burst of anger and denial, were determined to put things right.

A young attorney, Nelson Howarth, was initially defeated as a reform candidate for mayor in 1951—but he was elected in 1955. A group of reform-minded citizens, church and civic leaders, business people and electoral candidates walked neighborhoods to campaign for better schools and the money to pay for them, improved water quality, better police and fire protection and a crackdown on gambling and vice. They even asked for a new form of government for the city. They got everything they wanted, except the change of government, which came a generation later, in 1987, with the return to the alderman system abandoned in 1911.

So many positive changes in so short a time eventually won Springfield an All-American City

Saturday afternoon at the movies, in this case the old Roxy on South Fifth Street, was always a big favorite with children. A special free-admission day in 1948 drew a line all the way up the street.

prostitution and concentrated on economic conditions instead.

In the late 1930s and into 1940, uneasy citizens began to hear rumors of another war. But the bombing of Pearl Harbor in December 1941 and the country's entry into war turned all local attention away from civic improvement. Volunteer service was suddenly concentrated on raising war funds, scrap metal and grease drives and local Red Cross service. A gigantic munitions plant east of the city was a big employer and brought many new families to town, swelling the population. Housing

Aviation has fascinated Springfieldians ever since mobs welcomed "Birdman" Walter Brookins, who broke the world's record for continuous flight by flying from Chicago to Springfield in 1910. In the late 1920s, Lindbergh Field was opened (shown here). While some buildings from the old airfield are still standing today, activity shifted to Capital Airport after World War II.

designation in 1970.

But more than governmental changes were in the air in the 1950s and 1960s. Returning veterans and their families were desperate for housing. Dozens of new subdivisions opened up on all sides of town. Housing and commercial construction reached levels unheard of for generations. As the one- and then two-car family became common, the physical town spread out in every direction, with the heaviest growth to the southwest—a trend which had started in the early 1900s, when the large Butler and Leland family farms south of South Grand between Pasfield Street and Chatham Road began to be subdivided. The town, which had once clustered tightly in a few square miles around its public square, grew to over 10 square miles by 1950 and over 33 square miles by 1970. By 1990, it encompassed nearly 55 square miles. Physical growth was the greatest phenomenon, and the greatest problem of the half century following World War II. Once-self-contained towns like Rochester, Chatham, Sherman and Riverton began to have so many residents working and shopping in Springfield that they nearly became suburban Springfield themselves.

These physical changes, accompanied by a jump in population from a little over 80,000 in 1950 to over 103,000 in 1990, brought great social changes as well. The downtown would no longer function as Springfield's business and retail heart. As many left for new housing on the fringes of the city, some older neighborhoods deteriorated, often eroded by spot-zoned commercial intrusions. Expansion of the Capitol Complex and increasing traffic congestion meant the destruction of countless buildings and houses, many of them historic. A fledgling grass-roots preservation movement made its appearance in the 1980s in an attempt to stem the tide of destruction—a late arrival in a city which had long prided itself on its history. Incorporation of historic preservation into the fabric of the community was just one example of the overall need to plan for growth. By the start of the 1990s, Springfield dominated much of Sangamon County's landscape. Citizens became aware of a need to balance the desire for physical growth against the loss of farmland and costs to the environment.

In 150 years the community had become what early settlers had dreamed of, a thriving city of commerce, business and manufacturing, supported by a system of transportation beyond the pioneers' wildest hopes. Trains and streetcars were joined and superseded by airplanes and the private automobile. It was the automobile that worked the greatest change on the city's character, allowing growth to spread beyond what had once been imagined possible.

The future of the city of Springfield holds the promise for continued economic growth, as citizens concentrate on the challenges of keeping the city vital while addressing environmental, planning and social problems associated with that growth. Springfieldians of the past, through ambition, work, cooperation and sometimes even greed and corruption, gave us the city we now know. Springfield residents will continue to direct that same level of energy toward keeping it livable and functioning in the next century and beyond.

The 1950s saw the automobile change the face of every American city, and Springfield was no exception. The recent transformation of the city's geography made possible by the mall and shopping center had its roots in early suburban subdivisions like this one in Laketown, which originally stood in the middle of agricultural land.

2

Evolution of a Capital

DESTINY HAS ALWAYS SEEMED to favor Springfield as it has grown from a small nineteenth-century settlement on the banks of the Sangamon River. When the Sangamon declined as a source of commerce, chain links of railroads were there to service the lower Sangamon Valley, joined in twentieth century by U.S. Route 66 and a web of interstate highways. Together, they carried the pride of the prairie—its bounty and its people—to new economic high ground.

When the river provided insufficient water for the growing central Illinois hub of government and commerce, Lake Springfield came into being. Filling, almost miraculously, within a year, it became the wellspring for modern industrial growth. On its shore rose a large municipal electric plant that would become the envy of cities throughout the Midwest. A shoe factory, a flour mill and a bulldozer plant opened and thrived, and the prairie town grew along with them. When

"The growth on the West Side seems to have a force all its own," says Springfield's Mayor, Ossie Landfelder. This growth was given a huge boost in 1977, with the opening of the 1.1-million-acre White Oaks Mall.

external factors forced them to close their doors, Springfield hardly skipped a beat. The community, after all, had nurtured a growing, recession-resistant white-collar sector. As the seat of state government, Springfield and Sangamon County became the workplace for the finest physicians, engineers and lawyers in downstate Illinois.

From its inception in the 1820s as a classic farm community surrounding a bustling midtown square, Springfield became Illinois' third state capital in 1839 and sent a stooped, quaint-looking country lawyer off to serve in Washington 21 years later. It added a Civil War encampment for troops under the command of General Ulysses S. Grant. By the time Union soldiers came home, plans were being hatched to build a grand new State Capitol on a hill overlooking the heart of the city.

Even those who saw the new Capitol open in 1877 would have trouble recognizing its surroundings today. The Greater Springfield of today is a metropolitan area of 190,000 people. The city itself now covers more than 50 square miles. Its residents use 18 million gallons of water and 3,562 megawatts of electricity each day. Though still surrounded by rich farmland, it has given rise to several nearby communities—Chatham, Rochester, Riverton and Sherman among them—that have taken on the definite look of suburban America.

The area's diversified post-industrial economy

has not fared so badly, either. Its recent performance chart would demonstrate that recessions seem to happen only elsewhere. Greater Springfield, meanwhile, provides jobs for an estimated 120,000 people on any given working day. Sangamon County has never seen a jobless rate comparable to that of many parts of the Midwest. When the area's largest manufacturer closed its doors in 1985, the unemployment rate actually went *down*. And when building slumps hit the rest of the Midwest, capital from elsewhere seemed to find its way to Springfield, supporting growing banking and insurance companies, ongoing expansion at two major hospitals, a housing and commercial explosion on the city's West Side and a unique renaissance in downtown Springfield.

"Springfield, when I came here, was a very small community, one that didn't relate to being a capital city or a worldly city," says Mayor Ossie Langfelder, who arrived as a 14-year-old Austrian immigrant in 1940. "Today, we have grown up. We are the cosmopolitan, worldly city that the state capital of Illinois ought to be."

From its Lincoln-era historic sites to its imposing complex of government buildings, from its glittering lakeside college campuses to its churches, cultural activities and recreational opportunities, greater Springfield has matured far beyond its founders' vision. Few places are better prepared, its leaders uniformly believe, for the dawn of the twenty-first century.

NEIGHBORHOOD AND SUBURBAN DEVELOPMENT

The Springfield area is not without its economic problems, most noticeable among them a dwindling number of manufacturing jobs in a formerly industrialized city. An example is the shutdown of cake-mix and flour packaging operations at the Pillsbury Company facility on Springfield's North Side. Efforts by the Greater Springfield Chamber of Commerce and the Springfield and Sangamon County Economic Development Council continue in hopes of attracting big-ticket industrial employers, both from this country and overseas. Local officials recently reaffirmed interest in such prospects by adopting a new Springfield Comprehensive Plan that maintained a 500-acre site west of the city for major industrial development.

In the meantime, however, economic development programs operate on the premise that growth will come from within. There are plentiful examples of that premise in practice, and they are not isolated to any single locale within Sangamon County.

"People tend to focus on the West Side of

The Willard Ice Building is part of a master plan to fill the new downtown with office buildings, which the State of Illinois, for one, finds no trouble in filling.

town—the White Oaks area with its incredible growth—but we see plans for subdivisions and projects coming at us from all directions," says Henry Hopkins, the area's planning director. He doesn't exaggerate. How well has the evolution worked? How has the old river town weathered the currents that have buffeted less diversified communities in Illinois and around the country? Spin the compass. Economic activity can be found not only on the West Side, around the Capitol Complex or in downtown Springfield. But also the following.

CENTRAL SPRINGFIELD: A NEW FACE FOR THE FUTURE

The year was 1966, and downtown Springfield had not yet envisioned the changes that were about to shake the city's central business district to its historic foundations. Within the next decade, downtown would experience a dramatic exodus of department stores and specialty shops that was far from unique among midsize cities undergoing a mall-based suburban retail explosion. But something happened in 1966 that gave central Springfield a lease on life after retailing.

The decision was a democratic one. Heeding a referendum submitted to its employees, the insurance company Horace Mann Educators made the decision *not* to build a new headquarters on Springfield's far South Side. The specialty casualty insurer would instead erect a modern glass-and-steel home office between Seventh and Ninth streets, atop the rubble of old-town tenements. By doing so, it spawned a renaissance of decidedly ambitious proportions. For the next 25 years, hardly a season passed without construction cranes piercing the skyline of downtown Springfield. It became hard to find a block that the central city restoration movement had not left untouched.

Driven by strong municipal leadership and civic-minded involvement by organizations like the Springfield Central Area Development Association (SCADA), government and business have spent more than $295 million on downtown development and redevelopment since 1980. And all of it occurred within a half-mile of the Old State Capitol plaza. The entire area, once a typical Midwestern town square, has been transformed into a residential-tourist-office district whose tax base has grown, not declined, in the wake of the retail exodus.

"It happened because you had a lot of like-minded people who wouldn't give up on the area," says A. D. Van Meter, a retired bank executive, attorney and founding member of SCADA. "The important thing was that we didn't get fractured. We stayed together."

The silver-domed Capitol dominates the Springfield skyline. But lately it has had company, the distinctive round tower of the Springfield Hilton.

Though it resulted in considerable hand-wringing, there was no stopping the shift of retailing to the area around White Oaks Mall, on the city's far West Side. Within two years of the mall's opening, SCADA listed more than 70 vacant parcels of downtown property. Former mayor Mike Houston made redevelopment the cornerstone of his successful 1979 campaign, and civic leaders finally decided to capitalize on the assets the central area retained. With Horace Mann as an anchor to the east and the State Capitol Complex expanding to the west, Houston and others set about recasting the image of central Springfield. Though it was no longer where residents chose to shop, it would serve well as a place to work. And it could, with some effort, become an attractive place for people to live.

"It was like pulling teeth at first, but it was something we simply *had* to do," Houston recalls of early downtown renewal efforts. "It was not necessarily a matter of great vision for downtown, but a matter of numbers telling us what to do. For all practical purposes, downtown *is* your tax base, and the numbers told us that we couldn't afford to

allow the tax base to continue to decline."

Therefore, with state government as an interested partner, and with new tools like tax-free bonds and the existence of a Tax-Increment Financing District, project after project soon began to take shape. There were few, if any, failures along the way. An historic hotel would be gutted and outfitted with uptown apartments. A vacated department store would be converted into offices for a major state agency. A convention center would be built, and a 400-room luxury hotel would be constructed at its side. That was Phase One.

Phase Two would include a series of new brick office buildings along Madison Street, restoration of the old Union Station and development of Union Square Park immediately to the south. Suddenly, nearly 36,000 people were coming to work downtown each day. The Old Capitol and nearby Lincoln Historical District would continue to attract tourists. The State of Illinois would adopt a long-range plan that included not only the spacious Willard Ice Building, but also two other new office buildings, two parking structures and a landscaping plan that would give the Capitol Complex

There is more to downtown than offices, as this row of boutiques on Sixth Street attests.

and downtown Springfield a unified "Old Town" look.

Finally, there would be downtown's showpiece, Lincoln Square—the conversion of the entire block immediately south of the Old Capitol into a $13 million commercial and residential complex.

Michael Boer, president of the Greater Springfield Chamber of Commerce, was present for, and a party to, much of the change. But Boer, for one, still marvels at all that has happened to central Springfield.

"It was unbelievable, when you think about it," he says today, gazing out the window of his Lincoln Square office, which overlooks the Old Capitol. "I'm amazed and impressed by any number of things—the sheer number of projects, how far our renewal activity has spread, how much cooperation went into this and how easily this cooperation came about."

THE NORTH END: NO LONGER FOR ISOLATIONISTS

"Northenders," the saying goes, "live only to move into their parents' houses, patronize their own restaurants and bars, and hang out with the same folks with whom they shared elementary and high school experiences." There has been, over the years, a kernel of historical truth to isolationist tendencies among those who have spent their entire lives in the mix of ethnic communities represented in the bungalows around Lincoln and Fairview parks. But the North End, like the rest of Springfield, has out of necessity become a more open society. A decline in population has been curbed. A degree of gentrification can be observed, and families are moving in and out of the region with increasing regularity. There are, more important, major new economic factors in the North End and along the northern fringe of the city.

Capital Airport, for instance, handles more than 250,000 passengers a year and generates an estimated $508 million in economic activity, according to a recent Springfield Airport Authority study. "Outside of downtown Springfield, Capital Airport probably has the area's greatest potential for economic development," says Don Logue, a former local economic development executive and airport commissioner.

Once remotely positioned north of the city on a plain above the Sangamon River, the airport and its tenants now employ 2,700 people: the surrounding land may be as ripe for development as any within the borders of Sangamon County. For-

merly the nation's busiest all-commuter airport, the full-service aviation facility also saw scheduled jet service resume in late 1991. Traffic is forecast to continue its climb with completion of the Veterans Parkway beltway segment linking Capital Airport with the West and South sides of Greater Springfield. Airport commissioners, meanwhile, are being forced to discourage new residential growth in the area and have begun to seek new uses for acreage acquired as safety and noise-abatement "clear zones."

Additional potential has begun to be realized with approval of plans for a 40-acre business park between Veterans Parkway and the airport's cluster of runways. In addition, two neighborhood parks have been developed on airport land, and recent agreements have paved the way for a topflight, 18-hole golf course on rolling land north of the facility.

A rival to the development spurt around Capital Airport can be seen by backtracking east a bit along the Sangamon. A new bridge crosses the river on Business Route 55, near where I-55 bends east to bypass the city itself. Before long, planners may have reason to question why the four-lane bridge was built for existing needs only. The reasons relate to the homegrown growth climate in Williams Township (including the towns of Sherman and Williamsville), communities that rise to the north of Springfield along the I-55 corridor.

Sangamon County's first true bedroom community, Sherman has led the way as Williams Township's population nearly doubled to 2,800 between 1950 and 1990. Shopping plazas, supermarkets and a medical clinic opened to provide

Edwards Place, in the city's North End, built in 1833, is the home of the busy and thriving Springfield Art Association.

Sherman's high-income commuters with local services. The Rev. Peter Mascari held hundreds of chicken frys and bingo nights to realize his lifelong dream of building Villa Vianny, a full-service retirement community in Sherman. And prominent developer Leonard Sapp, himself a resident of the area, ended years of frustration by seeing half-million-dollar homes line the fairways of the Rail Golf club he built in the 1960s.

In Lincoln Park on the North End, laid out in the 1890s, a group finding exercise and enjoyment in tai chi is apparently oblivious to the passersby.

The Ladies Professional Golf Association holds a $500,000 women's professional golf tournament at the Rail, designed by legendary golf-course architect Robert Trent Jones. And Sherman, after years of patience, hopes soon to welcome Jumer's Castle Lodge, a multi-million-dollar luxury hotel and executive conference center between the Rail and Business Route 55.

"People are already starting to think about locating north of the river," says Hugh Garvey, a Williams Township developer and former mayor of Elkhart. "When people see them break ground for Jumer's, northern Sangamon County's really going to take off."

But as much as Capital Airport and Sherman have contributed to the North End's destiny, its most significant redevelopment can be found much nearer the State Capitol. A few blocks to the north is Goosetown. A neighborhood of German immigrants, its centerpiece, the Reisch Brewery, closed down in the 1960s. On its site today stands the Southern Illinois University School of Medicine, whose development has been part of an unstoppable expansion of Springfield's regional medical complex. S.I.U., along with St. John's Hospital on North Seventh Street and Memorial Medical Center on North First Street, have established

patient referral networks that cover more than 60 central and southern Illinois counties. The resulting growth has brought dozens of new medical office buildings and outpatient treatment centers into the once-quiet neighborhood.

"The medical centers have provided a solid foundation for sustained growth through the 1980s, and I see no evidence of the pattern changing," says Michael Boer of the Chamber of Commerce. "The importing of new dollars from the medical sector is just what the doctor ordered."

Because of its history and its residents' sense of place, the North End has developed other attributes over the years. Sangamon Center North offers modern retailing in the area, while North Grand Avenue is perhaps Springfield's most durable commercial strip. Edwards Place, operated by the Springfield Art Association, serves as a centerpiece for early gentrification efforts just north of the medical complex. Lanphier Ballpark is the home of the Springfield Cardinals of the Class A Midwest League. The rolling acres of Lincoln Park provide the neighborhoods with playgrounds, baseball fields, outdoor swimming and an indoor ice rink. Nearby, the Illinois State Fairgrounds, permanent home to the Illinois Department of Agriculture, hosts millions of visitors each year. They come to see major horse shows, auto and motorcycle races, an annual Ethnic Festival and, of course, the Illinois State Fair in early August.

WEST SIDE STORY: OLD TOWN REACHES FOR TOMORROW

Not long ago, while its denizens were still getting comfortable with the idea of a "new" State Capitol, Springfield became Illinois' fourth-largest city. After a brief midlife identity crisis, it graciously accepted big-city status.

The city's boundaries extended toward the Sangamon River to the north and east. Soon it would also have a large water impoundment, Lake Springfield, courtesy of the Depression-era Works Progress Administration, lengthening the city's shadows far to the south. However, a mile to the west of the new silver-domed State Capitol ran West Grand Avenue (today known as MacArthur Boulevard). Beyond it stood a convent, a coal mine, a few pig sties and very little else.

It would take until the mid-twentieth century for the cobblestones of progress to reach the western edge of sprawling Washington Park. And it would take another 50 years for the cornfields beyond to sprout ranch homes and TV antennas—and for west suburban·Springfield to be born.

Today, the farms have been pushed miles farther west. Chatham Road, once a gently rolling farm path and the city's invisible western boundary, now separates "old" and "new" West sides that are as different to each other as the eras during which they were developed. East of Chatham Road, stretching nearly from the Capitol Complex to Washington Park, are neighborhoods of tree-lined streets and stately two- and three-story houses, many dating back to the early 1900s. West of Chatham, stretching out along the fingers of Monroe and Washington streets and Wabash Avenue, there has been a multi-megaton explosion of housing, retailing, office and other commercial development in the past four decades.

The sons and daughters of people who rode streetcars out for day trips at Washington Park now stop at the park on their way home from work. More often, they snake along the wall-to-wall commercial channel that leads out MacArthur, turns south on Wabash and leads to the doorstep of the White Oaks Mall. "Amazing as it seems, over 75 percent of the net increase in population over the last 30 years has been west of Chatham Road," says Harry Hopkins, who has plotted most of the new

development during his 20 years as head of the Springfield-Sangamon County Regional Planning Commission: "The West Side has become the regional commercial center of central Illinois. We're in the infancy of office park development out there. And if we need a big industrial site for a new plant, it will be out there too."

Though he might have been impatient for awhile, Greeley today would be proud to see his advice being followed. The modern saga of Sangamon County expansion has been, quite simply, a West Side story.

So strong has been the growth climate, in fact, that no one knows where or when it will reach its peak. Still, 20 years after the boom was ignited, hardly a week goes by without new foundations being dug along the cul-de-sacs of a Harrison Park, a Koke Mill or a Grants Ridge, some of the newly developed subdivisions springing up west of Veterans Parkway (Illinois Route 4). Hardly a month passes without grand opening ceremonies for a new discount store, professional office complex or franchise restaurant. As the area's epicenter, meanwhile, White Oaks Mall is serving, conservatively, a 40-county trading area.

"People like to say they don't know where the money's coming from," says Hopkins. "I'll tell you where it's coming from—Jacksonville, Taylorville, Lincoln—anywhere within a 60-mile radius."

Comparisons are hard to establish, but West Side expansion indeed ranks among the most robust growth rates in the Midwest. Consider that the Midwest as a whole suffered a decline in population between 1980 and 1990, and that the 1980s were a break-even proposition in eight of Springfield's 10 wards. The city's two West Side wards were an entirely different story. Their population increased by 5,261 during the decade, equivalent to the net gain of the city as a whole.

"The growth on the West Side seems to have a force all its own. We can't see the end of it," says Springfield's Mayor, Ossie Langfelder. "I'm ecstatic about the prospects. What community leader

Apartments on the West Side have the homey charm you would expect from a thriving neighborhood in America's heartland.

Top: A close look at many of the old West End houses reveals charming architectural details.

Bottom: Southtown was first settled in the last century by German and Irish immigrants. Once the southern boundary of the city proper, it has retained its gracious character as the city has grown up around it.

wouldn't be?"

While it began as a housing boom, the West Side story took on much broader proportions with the opening of 1.1 million-square-foot White Oaks Mall in 1977.

By the time the bunting and balloons came down, the acreage at the northeast corner of Wabash and Veterans Parkway was well on its way to supplanting the old downtown square as the retail center of central Illinois. Melvin Simon Associates of Indianapolis had assembled four major department stores: Sears, Montgomery Ward, P. A. Bergner and, most notably, Famous-Barr of St. Louis. Around them opened more than the usual array of movie theaters, shoe stores, sportswear shops and booksellers. So strong has been the regional appeal that shoppers board White Oaks-bound buses from as far away as Decatur and Jacksonville, 40 miles to the east and west, respectively. And while White Oaks is twice the size of malls in typical midsize cities, it was not the end of the story. Rather, it signaled the beginning of a commercial migration to the West Side.

Soon, along the traffic pipeline to White Oaks, large gaps on MacArthur and Wabash would fill in with strip shopping centers, fast-food restaurants and furniture stores. Later, the approaches along Veterans from the north and south would be burgeoning along the same lines.

"We've gone through a period where anyone who was expanding in downstate Illinois wanted to open something on the West Side of Springfield," an area banker says. "I don't know of a stronger commercial real estate climate anywhere."

Adds developer Phil Spengler: "White Oaks is the magnet. Everyone wants to be near it."

The demand indeed has been insatiable. In the early 1990s, more than $300 million in new retail-office-industrial development was planned within a mile of White Oaks Mall. Most or all of the projects involved prominent local developers, each making a bid to capitalize on the area's newest asset: the long-awaited completion of the Central Illinois Expressway (U.S. Route 36), linking the West Side of Springfield with Jacksonville, Quincy and all of west-central Illinois.

The projects themselves promise even more diversification for the area. Barker Family Properties, which sold the land to White Oaks in the early 1970s, recently completed White Oaks West, a 335,000-square-foot retail center across Veterans Parkway to the west of the mall, and has pushed farther west along Wabash Avenue with the White Oaks West subdivision. At the southwest corner of Wabash and Veterans, meanwhile, developer Charles Robbins has leased out a large percentage of his 91-acre Southwest Plaza, which has attracted Phar-Mor Drugs and Best Buy discount outlets, as well as Sangamon County's first major suburban-style office park.

A half-mile farther south on Veterans, near its junction with the Central Illinois Expressway, Leonard Sapp & Associates has attracted the area's first Wal-Mart, Target, Menard's builders' supply and four motels to anchor its 170-acre Parkway Point development. Sapp's project also includes 26 acres set aside for light industrial development. With fast-growing Illini Technologies as its anchor tenant, the tract is expected to attract additional high-tech industries.

Population forecasters say West Side growth will continue, if at a somewhat slower rate, through the end of the year 2010. Gaps of undeveloped land are few on the West Side, so planner Hopkins says conversion of farm land farther to the west is likely to occur gradually. Already subdivisions are planned for much of the land in the mile between Koke Mill, just west of Veterans, and Meadowbrook Road, a mile farther west. Enhancing the area's appeal are completed segments of Veterans to Capital Airport and Illinois Route 29 and farther north to the Illinois State Fairgrounds.

Chris Dettro, business editor of the *State Journal-Register*, agrees that growth along the West Side Veterans corridor will continue unabated. "It's like a bathtub with the drain plug removed," he says. "No matter how hard you try to fill it up, there always seems to be room for more."

SOUTHTOWN AND BEYOND: A REGION RICH IN RESOURCES

Abraham Lincoln, circuit-riding lawyer, began and ended his tours at a clapboard two-story house on South Eighth Street. Though part of the Old Town of 1840, the clapboard-sided two-story was in something of a suburban site at the time, a circumstance that was about to change. Perhaps because of the famous 16th president (or perhaps in spite of his sometimes-unneighborly wife, Mary) an emerging mercantile class soon began erecting some of Springfield's finest homes on the south side of town, near what's now the tree-shaded Illinois Governor's Mansion, then called Aristocracy Hill.

Many of those same Victorian mansions, built as Springfield grew farther south in 1855 and again in 1857, still stand proudly today. Among the finest, stretching to South Grand Avenue along South Fifth, Sixth and Seventh streets—many now tastefully converted into professional offices—they serve as a long and sturdy stem for the growth and redevelopment activity that has mushroomed for miles beyond the grand old South Side neighborhoods.

Through the first half of this century, however, more profound economic forces rendered South Grand a useless barrier. By 1908, the city stretched nearly to the parkland that would become Bunn Park and would soon contain the city's first public golf course. Heavyweight legend Joe Louis made an appearance or two there. At about the same time, legend has it, nearby speakeasies just outside the city limits hosted summit conferences between the gangsters from upstate Chicago and their counterparts in Little Egypt, as southern Illinois was known at the time.

Since those days, however, South Grand and 11th Street, once the shady main streets of Southtown, have been widened into thick traffic arteries. Their purpose today: attaching central Springfield to a vast crescent of development that stretches beyond the distant shores of Lake Springfield and reaches far into southern Sangamon County.

The crescent encompasses City Water, Light & Power, Springfield's lakeside power generating station and waterworks, and serves as home to the expansive nearby campuses of Sangamon State University and Lincoln Land Community College. Bisected by Interstate 55, it contains Springfield's first shopping center (Laketown), its first mega-center (the recently renovated Capital City) and first and largest industrial park (Springfield Industrial Park). It attracts boaters and picnickers on summer weekends and visitors year-round, to an 1,800-room cluster of modern hotels anchored by the Holiday Inn East convention complex at I-55 and Adlai Stevenson Drive.

And while commercial and residential development hardly rivals the expansion to the west, census figures show that Springfield's First Ward, which encompasses much of the lake area, grew by 36 percent between 1980 and 1990. Meanwhile,

Bunn Park, in Southtown, is one of Springfield's many parks, offering large splashes of green and even a chance for a bit of fishing.

some of the area's most elegant estates have replaced the cottages and summer homes along the shores of Lake Springfield. Hundreds of new lots have been opened for development on land along the interstate and near the college campuses. And the once-sleepy farm towns of Rochester and Chatham, on the far shores of Lake Springfield, are sleepy no more, their collective population having tripled since 1950.

"The area has services and easy access, and its growth is about to accelerate," says Planning Commission director Hopkins.

What brought about the push beyond Southtown? Clearly, nothing rivals two monumental, if unrelated events of the mid-1930s. The first was a decision by a Wisconsin company known as Allis-Chalmers to buy the small Monarch Tractor manufacturing plant on South 11th Street near Bunn Park. The second was the move by the Depression-era Works Progress Administration to build an earthen dam at the confluence of Lick and Sugar creeks in 1935.

Allis-Chalmers, the area's industrial mainstay for the next 50 years, would vastly expand the tractor plant, building it into a city within a city that would employ 5,000 workers at its peak, on a 125-acre site strapped between South 11th and South Sixth streets. Before its shutdown in the 1980s under the subsequent control of Italian conglomerate Fiat, the plant would ship more than $200 million worth of construction equipment a year—including many of the machines touted as the "world's largest bulldozers."

Allis-Chalmers served an even more important purpose in the long-term development of Springfield and vicinity. True, it offered better-paying work to the denizens of old Southtown and created a new generation of two-room taverns for the after-work crowd. But the factory in its heyday also reached out for a work force in a way that has provided a lasting linkage between Southtown and smaller communities beyond Lake Springfield— Pawnee and Auburn as well as Rochester and Chatham.

While Rochester and Chatham have remained largely residential, the Pawnee-Auburn area, ironically, now represents the core of Sangamon County's residual manufacturing base. Pawnee, on the frontier of south-central Illinois' rich coal fields, is

home to 2,775 townsfolk and, significantly, to Peabody Coal's No. 10 Mine, still the world's largest underground mine. And most of Peabody's production nowadays travels but a short distance across Route 104—to a towering 1,108-megawatt Commonwealth Edison generating station that produces electricity which is then sent over high-voltage wires to supply the Chicago area.

Equipment of a high-tech variety comprises the output of the DICKEY-john Corporation, housed in a modern plant on the south edge of Auburn, population 5,082. A maker of digital instruments for farm combines and tractors, DICKEY-john and its 700-employee work force has succeeded Allis-Chalmers-Fiat as the area's leading industrial employer.

Interestingly, the future of the land beyond Southtown is deeply rooted in its past. Both Lake Springfield and the abandoned Allis-Chalmers property, the early pivot points for the region's development, have turned out to be the sites of major renewal efforts late in the twentieth century.

To the disdain of local cynics, a $2.5 million bond issue was floated in 1930 to build Lake Springfield—and it took the water impoundment less than a year to fill, in 1936. Since then, the lake's three major pools and 17.5-billion-gallon capacity have provided an ample water supply for two generations. Threats posed by recent droughts, however, have settled a 20-year debate and the city of Springfield is moving on the long-term development of a supplemental water supply. For years dubbed Lake II—now named Hunter Lake in honor of the late John Hunter, longtime city utilities commissioner—the new lake will hold an additional 15 billion gallons of water, easily accommodating a growth rate now pegged at 18 to 20 percent through the year 2010.

"Lake Springfield is one of the area's major assets, and we've always deemed the local water supply as more than adequate," says Chamber president Michael Boer. "Now, with Hunter Lake coming on-line, however, we have that much more firepower to go after major economic development targets."

Some of those targets, may well set up shop in a new, carefully planned office-industrial complex known as Park South. The project just so happens to be on a high-profile 125-acre tract between

Popeye's barbecue restaurant is one of the most popular draws on the East Side. It's not hard to imagine why!

> # The most impressive examples of redevelopment and civic renewal have come about over the last 10 years.

Sixth and 11th streets.

Purchased from Fiat for an estimated $7 million by a local group known as Sixth Street Developers and returned to raw land for $3 million which included city-supplied demolition funds, Park South is a fresh start for the Allis-Chalmers-Fiat site that was once the city and county's most productive property.

"It's by far the most exciting thing we've got going," says Mayor Langfelder, who has vowed to work toward the replacement of the community's lost manufacturing jobs. "There are abandoned factory sites like this throughout the Midwest. But the economy here is too strong, and the location is too good, to let that site go."

The *State Journal-Register's* Dettro says the $60 million Park South project will demonstrate exactly how strong the area's development climate can be. "It's a site that's been written off, more or less, since the last few years Fiat was operating there," he says. "Springfield has weathered so many declines, and weathered them so well, that this negative may result in a positive as well."

EAST SIDE: COMMUNITY OF PROMISE

Skirted by the Sangamon River and its flood plain, crisscrossed by railroad tracks that carried emigrés to the Land of Lincoln from the Mississippi Delta, the East Side of Springfield embodies both its biggest challenge and its brightest promise. Fanning north from Bunn Park to the working-class suburb of Grandview, reaching from the edge of downtown across the river to the Italian enclave that is the village of Riverton, the East Side is the Springfield of yesterday and, in many ways, the

Springfield of tomorrow.

"It's an area where the city has invested a lot of money in community development programs and infrastructure improvements," says Michael Farmer, economic development director of the Greater Springfield Chamber of Commerce. "Fortunately for us, those investments are starting to pay off."

Consider, for instance, that the East Side, perhaps for the first time since the turn of the century, has begun to experience noticeable growth in recent months and years. From the high-rise apartment buildings and grand new brick office buildings in the corridor between East Capitol and East Madison streets to the new car fleets and glass-and-steel government complexes along Dirksen Parkway, the region's contributions to the Springfield-area economy are many and often underrated. "It's an area that can't grow much physically because of the river and its flood plain," says Hopkins. "But it's an area that is continuing to fill in on the land that is available."

The most impressive examples of redevelopment and civic renewal have come about over the past 10 years immediately to the east of downtown Springfield. Nearly a dozen new office buildings have sprung up from parking lots and weed patches along Ninth and Eleventh streets, the showpieces among them being the editorial and business offices and printing plant of the *State Journal-Register*, Illinois' oldest daily newspaper, and the spanking new Sangamon County Center, a $45 million project that covers most of a city block and contains modern courtrooms, government offices and a high-tech 280-inmate jail. Meanwhile, a succession of parks, greenbelts and recreational facilities rest alongside the city's new Jefferson-Madison corridor, once the site of Springfield's most blighted housing. And finally, a new generation of urban dweller has begun to appear among the neighbors of Pioneer Park, a middle-class subdivision being developed on land cleared 20 years ago through city and federal urban renewal efforts.

The larger East Side covers land stretching from central Springfield to the Sangamon River. From an economic development standpoint, it has a rich history. Bank One, Springfield, central Illinois' largest financial institution, started out in life as Marine Insurance Company, insuring many of the rural products that moved from point to point on flat-bottomed boats. Although no longer commercially navigable, the Sangamon once carried a wide assortment of

The modern offices of the *State Journal-Register*, Springfield's hometown paper with a statewide reach.

goods as it meandered past nineteenth-century settlements like Decatur, Springfield and Lincoln's boyhood home of New Salem.

No doubt because of the river, transportation systems have remained the lifeblood of commerce and development on the East Side and eastern suburban Springfield. As river commerce slowed, a web of railroads cut rights-of-way through the area: first the Illinois Central, then the Gulf, Mobile and Ohio, Chicago & Illinois Midland and Norfolk-Southern. Their importance can be measured, among other ways, by the fact that their tracks remain active along corridors that represent Third, Eleventh and Nineteenth streets. And while the number of urban manufacturers and shippers has declined in recent years, the East Side railroads nonetheless carry huge volumes of farm products, coal and petrochemicals. Their legacy is an arc of warehouses and small shipping concerns that dot Springfield's East Side.

Modern-day growth, too, has its roots in transportation networks. In addition to housing a cadre of small but growing minority-owned businesses, the East Side hosts a number of small manufacturers like Nudo Products (a profitable maker of poly-covered wall board) and Thompson Kitchens (one of the nation's fastest-growing packagers of dietetic products), largely because of easy access to rail and truck transport routes.

Among the more recent successes, from Farmer's standpoint, are industrial and commercial complexes that have sprung up around each of three East Side interchanges on Interstate 55. The Chamber of Commerce and its Economic Development Council led the way by negotiating with A.B.F. trucking concern for the location of a sprawling new spiderweb terminal alongside I-55 at Sangamon Avenue. With its arrival in the mid-1980s, A.B.F. added more than 650 jobs to the local economy and served as an anchor for an industrial complex that includes Central States Coca-Cola, a pair of heavy-equipment dealerships and several other enterprises.

But growth at I-55 and Sangamon, on the city's far Northeast Side, is but the latest example of commercial development in the narrow ribbon of land between I-55 and Dirksen Parkway. Once the bypass for U.S. Route 66 around Springfield (renamed in honor of the late U.S. Senator Everett McKinley Dirksen), the Dirksen Parkway of today has become a heavily traveled four- and five-lane strip that leads from Sangamon Avenue to the large, campuslike government complexes of the Illinois Department of Transportation and the Illinois Secretary of State's Office. Two of the largest state agencies in Springfield, they employ more

than 2,500 workers, many of them professional engineers and planners who oversee projects ranging from rural intersection improvements to a third major airport for metropolitan Chicago.

It is alongside Dirksen, too, that 80 percent of the area's new cars—and a majority of its used-car fleet—are polished up and displayed under bright

lights. The dealerships extend several blocks to the north and south of the J. C. Penney Company complex at South Grand and Dirksen, an area that has recently begun to attract roadside hotel development as well.

One interchange to the north, where K-Mart set up its first Springfield-area outlet, the wrecking ball has toppled the rickety wooden grandstand of the old Springfield Speedway. In place of the Sunday night midget auto races, developer Ralph Hurwitz has attracted new neighbors for K-Mart, including an East Side Bank One branch, several new restaurants and other roadside businesses.

Even the farm fields beyond Dirksen Parkway, beyond I-55, participated in the growth climate that engulfed Springfield during the 1980s. The communities of Clear Lake and Riverton townships, which straddle Interstate 72 as it moves east from Springfield, have doubled in population since 1950, according to 1990 Census Bureau accounts. While still the slowest-growing sector of the county, the wooded, rolling countryside and bluffs overlooking the Sangamon offer scenic and attractive home sites. They are expected to continue to attract small-scale residential growth through the end of the century.

Springfieldians have been baseball crazy for at least 70 years. Lanphier Park is home to the Class A Springfield Cardinals farm team, which keeps up a 70-game schedule from April through August.

3

Strengths of Commerce

HE FIRST SETTLERS TO the area known as the Sangamon Country built their rough-hewn homesteads along the banks of Spring Creek in about 1818. Among those earliest immigrants was Elisha Kelly, a North Carolinian, who was so taken with the beauty and bounty of the surrounding countryside he persuaded his father, four brothers and several friends from North Carolina to join him in the move west.

The Kelly settlement prospered and in 1821 became the seat of government in the newly organized Sangamon County. Not long after, a 25-year-old Kentuckian, Elijah Iles, moved in and made his mark as the county's first businessman.

When Iles arrived in the area late in the spring of 1821, he moved in with one of the Kellys until his business, a dry-goods store, was completed. The store was located near what is now Second and Jefferson streets in Springfield. Iles had to travel to St. Louis for supplies for his new business. His first supply list included $1,500 worth of groceries, wrought

Looking almost like figures in a Renaissance fresco, a group of craftsmen pauses in its work restoring one of Springfield's historic churches.

iron, pot metal and dry goods which he paid for and shipped back up the Illinois River to Beardstown.

Since there were no direct water routes to his new home in the middle of the prairie, the goods had to be transported cross-country to Springfield before he could set up his shop.

Springfield's first retail establishment served the basic needs of the nine families who lived within its two-mile radius.

The settlement, which soon became one of the largest communities between Chicago and St. Louis, was in the right place, it seemed. Its selection as the state's capital in 1837, historians say, cemented its claim to rapid growth and secured its status in the marketplace.

The population burgeoned from 4,500 in 1850 to nearly 25,000 in 1890. New railroad lines, the iron arteries of the developing economy, brought the raw materials of production into the city and carried millions of tons of coal, grain and manufactured goods to the rest of the country.

Springfield Iron Works was organized in 1871 to produce iron and steel rails for the emerging railroad industry. Tons of bituminous coal, discovered in the 1850s near Riverton (east of Springfield), provided fuel for iron works. Coal from the Beard-Hickox Coal Company, whose mine was a scant 200 yards from Springfield Iron Works, fed the giant fires of the mill.

Illinois was among the top coal producing states in the late 1800s, second only to Pennsylvania. Rich veins of coal stretched for miles beneath the verdant prairie of west central Illinois. At one

Illini Technology has grown by basing itself on the future, which lies in part in the high-tech computer industry.

point there were some 35 active mines in the county, twenty of them in and around Springfield. New fortunes were made as Springfield capitalists threw their cash behind coal-mining ventures.

Seventy million tons of coal a year were being taken from the mines in the 1890s. During World War I, Sangamon County earned second place in coal production in the state.

Coal mining, manufacturing and agriculture were the primary means by which the people of the area earned their livelihoods through the late nineteenth century and well into the twentieth.

While laborers mined the ore from the region's underground fuel reserves, farmers plowed under towering prairie grasses to plant corn and wheat. Agriculture flourished in a region where the soil was—and is—considered to be some of the richest in the country. Broad expanses of prairie grass and plants, some said to be tall enough to hide a man on horseback, covered the prairie and sent roots down into the rich loess.

So that more fields could be planted, thick stands of white and sugar maple, hickory, ash, walnut and oak were cleared from the flood plains stretching out from Horse Creek, Sugar Creek, Lick Creek and the snaking Sangamon River.

According to one citizen's account: "Little vacant land is to be found in any part of the county and almost every acre is under cultivation. The corn crop never fails, wheat seldom, and all other kinds of grain and fruit do well."

As agriculture became more and more productive, land values soared. New industry arose to support the farm work. Specialized equipment that allowed the ground to be broken more easily was developed by local manufacturers, and agriculture began to contribute to the wealth of local residents.

The city took its first step toward the formal promotion of local business in 1869. The Springfield Board of Trade, the city's first economic development organization, concentrated its efforts on luring new manufacturers, touting the city's numerous rail lines and able work force. Nearly a million dollars was invested in manufacturing over the next few years.

With the help of the Board of Trade, the Illinois Watch Factory, Ide's Engine Works, the Excelsior and Aetna foundries, Springfield Rolling Mills, boiler works and agricultural implement makers grew into productive businesses. At the turn of the century, Springfield had 320 manufacturing businesses representing more than $5 million in capital investment and employing more than 3,500 workers.

In only four score and three years, Springfield had changed from a small rural settlement where

Top: Lunchtime brings office workers out to enjoy the sun and shade of Old Capitol Plaza downtown.

Bottom: Poring over blueprints at the Springfield engineering firm of Crawford, Murphy & Tilley, founded in 1946.

Top: Locals claim that Springfield is a "recession-proof" city, which means that its citizens are busy building even when much of the rest of the country is pulling in its horns.

Right: The A.B.F. trucking company is an important business anchor of Springfield's East Side, the site of its relatively new spider-web terminal, conveniently situated alongside Interstate 55.

hunting and trade provided economic sustenance to a regional center of commerce and government.

Manufacturing played an important role in the lives of thousands of area residents during the first half of the twentieth century, spurred in part, by the demands of a wartime economy. Industrial employers like Sangamo Electric, Weaver Manufacturing, Pillsbury Mills and the International Shoe Company shipped their products throughout the country.

But even as the manufacturers absorbed the financial benefits of a healthy postwar economy, the face of Springfield's work force began to change. As the city grew and state government expanded, Springfield put on a white collar. Insurance, education, medicine and government began to employ an ever greater percentage of the work force.

By the mid-1980s, Springfield's ancestral manufacturers, Allis-Chalmers (Fiatallis), Sangamo Electric, Pillsbury Mills, Weaver Manufacturing and the International Shoe Company had either closed or moved out of the city.

In a sense, the demolition of Fiatallis's massive manufacturing complex represented the final metamorphosis of the city's heavy industry sector.

A 123-acre industrial complex that once provided employment for two generations of workers was dismantled, every trace swept from the landscape by giant earth-moving tractors similar to the ones Springfield workers had assembled on the site for decades. New red masonry gates mark the entrance to the yet undeveloped site. Soon, Park South, a multi-use commercial development under the guidance of a group known as Sixth Street Developers, will add yet another page to the history of business and industry in Springfield.

Park South is expected to offer something for everyone. Retail stores, upper-end offices and light manufacturing concerns are high on the list of prospective tenants. Two strip shopping centers are also planned for the southern third of the developments each anchored by a major retail store.

While Springfield's economic ups and downs sometimes mirrored those of the nation over the years, the overall impact of a downturn has been less severe. Many in the area believe the city is essentially recession-proof. The key to its success seems to be the diversity of employment opportunities. Government and related businesses, medicine, insurance and professional services have proven to have been a perfect mix of options when the recessionary waves have dashed the nation's economy.

Michael Ayers, associate professor of economics at Sangamon State University and a member of the Springfield Economic Development Council, says that Springfield's economy, with its extensive medical community, several institutions of higher education and a deeply rooted financial-insurance industry, helps the city to weather most economic trials.

"These institutions employ a tremendous number of people. A downturn in one area is less likely to hurt the local economy where there is adequate diversity," Ayers said.

Today the Springfield area employs more than 120,000 people. The work force is relatively young, with the heaviest concentration of employees in the 35 to 44 age range.

In recent years, per capita income in Sangamon County increased by 58 percent, exceeding the national growth rate of 56 percent and the state's rate of 52 percent.

The city's central location, 190 miles south of Chicago and 100 miles northeast of St. Louis, with convenient access by Interstate Highways 55 and 72, or by rail or air from Chicago or St. Louis, makes Springfield all the more attractive for residents and visitors.

Government, while smaller in size than in the decades of the 1970s and 1980s, continues to provide employment for approximately 32 percent of all jobs in the greater Springfield area.

Service-related industries provide 25 percent of the jobs, manufacturing only about 4 percent, and retailing about 20 percent. Hospitals and other medical facilities employ nearly 5 percent.

Insurance and financial institutions account for approximately 7.8 percent of all jobs in Springfield.

The financial district, which includes two

Garrett Aviation Services is one of the many secondary enterprises situated in and around Capital Airport.

national insurance companies, several banks and national brokerage firms, surrounds the Old State Capitol, and provides a firm anchor for the city as it continues to grow to the south and west.

Springfield's first bank, State Bank, was established in 1830, and failed shortly thereafter. In 1851, Clark's Exchange Bank was organized by N. H. Ridgely, who purchased the interests of his partners 15 years later and renamed the bank Ridgely National Bank.

Springfield Marine and Fire Insurance Company's bank was chartered in 1851 by Jacob Bunn, a wholesale and retail grocer, as an insurance company with banking privileges. The bank, which later became Marine Bank of Springfield and is now part of the Bank One Illinois network, has lived up to its legacy as a customer-service establishment. As the story goes, when Springfield Marine failed in 1878, Jacob Bunn resolved to repay his customers' losses personally. His heirs

The poinsettias at Buckley Greenhouses show the "green" face of enterprise in Springfield.

inherited the responsibility and paid the debt, even though it took until 1925. Although the bank's offices have moved several times over the years, its imposing Banking Hall, located between Adams and Washington streets, still casts a long shadow over the Old State Capitol Building, where Abraham Lincoln made his famous "House divided against itself" speech.

John Williams, who migrated from Kentucky to Illinois in 1823 and bought Elijah Iles's store, was among the city's first merchants and bankers. He served as a director in the Springfield branch of the Illinois State Bank and later was one of the incorporators of Springfield Marine and Fire Insurance Company, the predecessor of Marine Bank. In the late 1860s, with a good deal of business experience and an accumulation of personal wealth, he started his own bank, which was called Illinois National Bank. Today, First National Bank, the direct descendant of the original Illinois National, remains the only locally owned bank in Springfield, with $485 million in assets.

First of America Bank, with assets of $650 million, also has deep footings in the economic and cultural life of Springfield. The bank's roots go back to 1886, when it was called the Illinois National Bank. During the 1980s, Illinois National became part of Midwest Financial Group, Inc. In 1990, First of America Corporation bought out Midwest Financial. Today, First of America employs some 350 people in Springfield and another 100 people in two neighboring cities. The bank's employees take the city's quality of life very seriously, and Richard K. McCord, First of America's president, encourages them to become leaders in Springfield's numerous cultural and charitable organizations.

One of the city's first insurance groups was founded by seven central Illinois businessmen who gathered at the Leland Hotel in downtown Springfield on March 4, 1884. The group assembled for "the purpose of considering a plan upon which to organize a new life association." Membership in Franklin Life Association would be open to "all MALE persons who ... pass a proper medical examination, between the ages of 21 and 55 inclusive," with some "occupational exceptions." According to the minutes, founders R. L. McGuire, J. R. Miller, H. C. Feltman, B. M. Griffith, Henson Robinson and E. P. House, decided that "no applications for membership in this association will be accepted from persons who live south of the northern boundary line of Tennessee."

The Franklin quickly outgrew its first home, in the Hay Building, and the directors authorized construction of new premises at the corner of Fifth

and Monroe streets. Construction costs topped $100,000 by the time the building was completed, but it served as Franklin Insurance Company's home office from 1893 until 1913. The company then moved into the first four-story unit at its current site, on the block bordered by South Sixth and Seventh streets, near downtown.

The Franklin maintains its home office complex in Springfield, employing 1,368 people. The company's assets totaled $5 billion in 1992 and with its cadre of 3,000 sales associates provides service to one million policy owners throughout the United States.

Springfield also serves as the headquarters for the insurance holding company, Horace Mann Educators Corporation, founded in 1945. Today, the company is a multi-line insurance company with $2.5 billion in assets, serving the educational community. The home office employs 1,400 locally.

From Elijah Iles's first dry-goods store to the present day, Springfield has served as a regional hub for retail shopping. In Springfield, it seems, there is always room for one more retailer. Retail sales in the county have increased each year since 1980—more than 50 percent in a decade.

The Springfield trade area is supported by

more than 213,000 households with an effective buying income of approximately $6.3 billion. Sales per capita averaged $12,732 in 1991, according to state Department of Revenue figures. There are 15 major shopping areas in Springfield, the largest of which is White Oaks Mall, the regional shopping center completed in 1977.

While some critics have said that regional malls drain retail business out of downtown areas, others give them credit for spurring the redevelopment of neighborhood shopping oases and the renovation of aging city centers. Springfield's neighborhood shopping centers, many refurbished and updated, have proved to be the salvation of many busy households. Restaurants, drugstores, movie rental shops and grocery stores provide easy access and convenient parking.

The Old State Capitol and grounds are the centerpiece around which Springfield's downtown business district has redesigned itself. Clothing stores, movie theaters and many of the city's grand contingent of stately old hotels may have retired from downtown, but the city has worked hard to transform its empty storefronts into boutiques, art galleries, offices and apartment buildings.

Downtown is the place to go for housing, an

A customer consults in a branch of the First National Bank, one of Springfield's leading financial institutions.

array of restaurants, bars, jazz clubs and businesses. In addition to the major banks located in the downtown area, brokerage firms, law offices, state, county and city offices provide a central location for commerce.

The city's tourism office is located downtown, across the street from the convention center, which also serves as an entertainment hub for city residents and thousands of visitors and conventioneers throughout the year.

Located just south of downtown is one of Springfield's most renowned engineering firms, Hanson Engineers. Organized by Walter E. Hanson and a group of engineers in 1954, the firm provides geotechnical, structural and transportation engineering, environmental and waste-management services, hydrologic and hydraulic engineering, and material testing for clients throughout the United States and the world.

One of the more significant projects the company is responsible for is the 4,620-foot, cable-stayed bridge across the Mississippi River. The three-span bridge was designed to carry U.S. 67 from Alton, Illinois, to St. Charles County, Missouri.

> ## The local economy has flourished because it has continuously evolved and pursued economic diversity.

The engineering firm of Crawford, Murphy & Tilly Inc. (C.M.T.), founded in 1946 by Len Crawford, James Murphy and Ray Tilly, has continued to grow and prosper. Today the 200-employee firm has offices in Springfield, Aurora and St. Louis and ranks 279 among the country's top 500 firms, according to *Engineering News Record* magazine. The firm specializes in aviation, hydraulics, highways, environmental, architectural, structural and electrical-mechanical work. In 1990 and 1991, C.M.T. won the "Eminent Conceptor Award," the highest award presented through the Consulting Engineers Council of Illinois' Engineering Excellence Awards Competition.

General construction in Sangamon County increased dramatically during the second half of the 1980s, and local officials are confident that the long trend will continue.

Residential development grew by an additional one million square feet of living space each year at the end of the 1980s. The average sale price for a home in Springfield was $80,799 in 1992, according to the Springfield Association of Realtors. The strongest demand for houses in the late 1980s and into the 1990s was in the $100,000 to $125,000 range.

Home resale activity in Springfield has soared so far in the 1990s. Two hundred more units were sold through July 1992 than through the first seven months of 1991, a 15.6 percent increase. Dollar volume for the first seven months of 1992 totaled $131.38 million, a 22.4 percent increase over 1991.

While low mortgage rates played a role in the volume of homes sold, wide-ranging job opportunities, beautiful parks and excellent educational facilities in the city attract hundreds of new residents every year.

In addition to new residents, the city also fares well with tourists. Tourism, one of the fastest growing segments of

Downstate Illinois is fundamentally an agricultural part of the state. Combines harvest corn almost at Springfield's doorstep.

the state's economy, contributes to the stability of the local economy as well. Local tourism officials report that visits to major historic sites in Springfield were up significantly, in spite of a slow start in the summer of 1992.

Tourism contributes millions of dollars annually to Springfield's economy. Spending by conventioneers exceeded $50 million in 1991.

Millions come to visit Abraham Lincoln's home, the Old State Capitol, Lincoln's Tomb in Oak Ridge Cemetery, the State Capitol Building, the poet Vachel Lindsay's home, the newly restored Dana-Thomas House by Frank Lloyd Wright, historic churches, beautiful architecture and parks each year. The total number of visitors to local historic sites increased by three percent to 2.2 million in 1992.

The Springfield Convention & Visitors Bureau is responsible for marketing and promoting the city's famous landmarks and natural beauty for conventions, meetings, trade shows, tour groups and individuals visiting the area.

According to recent statistics, the average group of travelers to the city is likely to spend nearly $170 on their visit. Tourism boosts hotel and motel sales figures and contributes significantly to the fortunes of city restaurants and retail establishments.

The Greater Springfield Chamber of Commerce, the Economic Development Council, the city's economic development department and the state Department of Commerce and Community Affairs work together to retain and enhance the business climate and to develop new opportunities.

"There's a lot of momentum in the Springfield economy," said Michael Boer, president of the Greater Springfield Chamber of Commerce. "There are always projects on the drawing board."

And in order to sustain the growth that Springfield has been so successful at achieving, the Chamber and other economic development organizations are now aggressively pursuing regional economic development as a means of retaining business interests and attracting new and related

industries to the region.

Michael Ayers of Sangamon State University notes that the day-to-day efforts of the agencies' workers are key to maintaining a healthy economic mix. "They are the workhorses," he said. "Every year 600 to 700 jobs are created as a result of their efforts. They look for funding sources, they search for job training programs to assist those out of work, they try to match services with need. There is little to be gained by pitting city against city in a race to capture a business. There is everything to be gained by cooperating, and maybe everyone is better served."

Ayers added: "Companies don't see city boundaries, so why should we? We need to look beyond our borders."

Pride in workmanship and accomplishment is evident in this Springfield baker, who poses with his creations.

4

The Seat of Government

N 1837, A LANKY 28-YEAR-OLD state legislator led a similarly tall delegation of Sangamon County lawmakers in capturing a prize that had far-reaching repercussions for their county seat. The "Long Nine," as the two senators and seven representatives were called—their collective height was 54 feet— stood even taller back home after persuading the General Assembly to designate Springfield as Illinois' permanent state capital. Upon hearing the news, the bustling frontier town of 1,100 erupted into raptures. Joyful citizens built a huge bonfire around the whipping post on the public square. The Long Nine, whose number included the Whig Party's able floor-leader, Abraham Lincoln, were the heroes of the day.

But even as the glow of victory faded, leaders in the state's new capital city were recognizing that the honor carried weighty new responsibilities. The *Sangamo Journal's* editor, Simeon Francis, wrote with cautious opti- mism of his hope for the prairie town "that every class of our

A view of the inside of the famous silver dome of the Illinois State Capitol Building, completed in 1877.

Advice and consent some-
times take place informally
within the State Capitol.

The imposing interior of the
Illinois House of Representatives. The ceiling is especially
beautiful.

citizens look to the future with confidence that we trust will not be disappointed." And the future U.S. Senator Stephen A. Douglas proposed a magnanimous toast to his newly adopted city: "The last winter's legislation—may its results prove no less beneficial to the whole state than they have to our town."

Partisans of other cities may still debate the benefits that Springfield's standing as Illinois' capital city holds for them. But there is little doubt that the "Little Giant" was correct in assessing the impact of the new status on Springfield. After more than 150 years as Illinois' capital, Springfield and its vicinity owe much to the Long Nine.

"Being the capital city of Illinois places us among some of the most important cities of the nation, if not the world," says Springfield Mayor Ossie Langfelder. "We owe much to that standing, and we owe much of that standing to our history and traditions."

As Illinois' government has grown and spread through the city, Springfield and its surrounding areas have prospered in an economy anchored firmly in tax-funded services. Government is the chief industry of Sangamon County and a major player in the economies of each adjoining county.

During 1992, the public sector employed nearly a third of the workers in the two-county Springfield Market Service Area.

In other words, almost 35,000 of the 109,000 available jobs in Sangamon and Menard counties were payrolled by government. And the vast majority of those workers, about 23,500, received bimonthly paychecks cut by the state comptroller. With an average income of approximately $30,500 annually, these predominantly white-collar wage earners injected more than $700 million into the local economy. They also helped keep the region's unemployment rate below national and state averages.

Apart from its financial contribution, the region's largest employer colors almost every aspect of life in Springfield. The impact of state government is apparent throughout the city, whether one's view is turned toward the cityscape or to the types of people, related industries and wealth of state services to be found there.

Another significant player in the region's economy is local government, which accounted for about 9,000 jobs during 1992 in Sangamon and Menard counties. The recently reorganized Springfield city government employs about 1,650, about 700 of whom work for the municipal utility, City Water, Light & Power. An additional 250 are employed by other city governmental units, including the Springfield Park District, Housing

Authority and Metropolitan Sanitary District.

Sangamon County's government also makes its home in Springfield. Most of the 560 county employees are based in a distinctive red-brick jail-courthouse complex, completed in 1991 at a cost of about $45 million.

Rounding out the public sector is federal government, with about 2,275 employees in the Springfield region. While the Lincoln Home National Historic Site is the best-known federal presence in Springfield, Illinois National Guard units actually account for the largest contingent of federal workers. The U.S. government also can be seen in a major regional post office, an Internal Revenue Service district office and a host of agricultural agencies.

In all, public service is one of the state capital's most important enterprises. As such, it has promoted the existence of a relatively well-paid, professional class of citizens and the ready availability of an array of government services.

STATE GOVERNMENT

Often described as a "city within a city," the Capitol Complex has actually become less distinct from the rest of Springfield over the years. The statehouse, rising 405 feet above the surrounding prairie and visible for miles, is the most recognizable and enduring symbol of state government in Springfield. But the steady growth of state government, particularly with the explosion of services in the 1930s has pushed one administrative agency after another from the Capitol Building into roomier quarters.

State government now occupies nearly half the office space downtown, and many agencies have established permanent outposts near the highways on the city's outskirts. Trade organizations and businesses that count state government among their chief clients have followed suit.

Upon its arrival in Springfield, Illinois' government made its home in a Greek Revival-style statehouse with massive sandstone pillars and a colonnaded wooden dome. The two-story structure, set in the center of the town's public square, was designed to house all of state government under a single roof. That proved to be a convenient plan, for early visitors to Illinois' first permanent capital reported that the city's streets were mired in mud and overrun with hogs.

But state government quickly outgrew its new quarters. In 1867, the legislature authorized construction of a far larger and considerably more elaborate statehouse. Springfield fended off attempts by other communities to lure away the capital, and 1877 saw the General Assembly convene its first session in the sprawling new Capitol Building. By the summer of 1888, the fabulous sum of $4.5 million had been spent on the grand Italianate structure. Like its predecessor, the new pillared and porticoed statehouse was designed to house all of state government. But as the state's need for additional office and storage space continued to expand, one agency after another left the Capitol to establish new headquarters at increasingly distant locations.

A look back through the editions of the Springfield-Sangamon City Directory attests to both the growth of state government and the exodus from the Capitol. In 1900, the city directory listed 21 state government offices. All those agencies, down to the now-defunct State Board of Livestock Commissioners, listed addresses in the Capitol. By 1935, the number of state government listings had grown to 122, and the web of state services had extended to several new locations, including the recently built Centennial Building. By 1990, the directory offered 168 state listings with addresses in virtually every section of town.

A recent study by the Springfield-Sangamon County Regional Planning Commission brings an even sharper focus to the state's presence in Springfield. The 1985 survey found that the state owned more than 2.5 million square feet of offices and leased an additional 1.4 million square feet, mostly in the central business district. Altogether, state agencies occupied about 45 percent of the office space identified in the survey.

And by late 1992, state government was renting more space than it owned, with contracts to lease close to 3.7 million square feet of Springfield office space, most of it from Springfield-based landlords. Many a vacant or under-utilized downtown office building or closed store has found new life as a state administrative center.

Despite this process of spreading out, the silver-domed Capitol Building remains the hub of state government in Springfield. Its space is now

The seal of the State of Illinois, whose capital has been located in Springfield for more than 150 years.

The silver-domed Capitol Building remains the hub of state government in Springfield.

reserved primarily for the deliberations of the General Assembly and as headquarters for five of the state's six elected constitutional officers. Only the attorney general's offices are located in an auxiliary building, just southeast of the Capitol. Both the House of Representatives and the Senate maintain chambers and leadership offices on the third floor, and members vie for office space nearby. Some legislators have their offices in the William G. Stratton Building, just west of the Capitol.

As both landlord and tenant, state government has been a good neighbor to Springfield residents.

The cluster of 27 buildings in the Capitol Complex is carefully maintained, and their grounds display the dedicated attention of a corps of landscape gardeners. A major new addition to the complex was completed in 1990 with the opening of the Illinois State Library, just east of the Capitol Building. And a series of other capital improvements is well under way. A comprehensive plan adopted in 1988 calls for a total of $129.1 million in spending to improve traffic flow, add office space and provide additional parking. A key component of the plan pledges the state to honor streetscaping standards adopted by the city of Springfield. Over time, this provision will ensure an uninterrupted flow of brick sidewalks lighted by wrought-iron street lamps from the central business district to the Capitol Complex.

But apart from a massive and unmistakable presence on the skyline of the Greater Springfield region, state government also has a profound impact on the local economy and on the texture and quality of its social and cultural life. City historian Ed Russo likens Springfield's wedding its fortunes to state government to a Victorian maiden who has snared an impressive catch: "True, the match gave Springfield an assured social position as an important city, financial ease as politicians, office-seekers, hotel-keepers, lawyers and physicians flocked to the new capital, and countless diversions in the form of levees, balls and social intrigue. But all of this was at a cost to her character development apart from being the site of Illinois government.

"Holding together this marriage with state government was full-time work for Springfield well into the twentieth century as other rivals—Peoria and Chicago, especially—sought to wrest away the prize. It required constant vigilance and a willingness to cater to government's exhausting demands for working space, dining, housing, entertainment—and, more recently, parking—for those laboring in service."

That process has had a profound impact on Springfield's development, and its residents, like most Victorian ladies, seemed content with their "match."

As the seat of government for the nation's sixth most populous state, Springfield is a major hub for decision makers. By law, all six elected state constitutional officers must maintain a Springfield residence. The Executive Mansion serves not only as the First Family's home, but also as a gracious setting for state receptions and dinners. In recent years, the meticulously landscaped mansion grounds, just east of the Capitol, have been the setting for an annual antiques show, attracting vendors from throughout the Midwest. And at Halloween, costumed school children have grown accustomed to trick-or-treating the governor himself.

During the Illinois General Assembly's legislative sessions each spring and fall, the city and its inns are thronged with the state's 177 legislators, their staffs and representatives of hundreds of organizations that follow the lawmakers' activities. During the 1992 legislative session, 863 lobbyists were registered to do business with the legislature. Many of the organizations they represent maintain year-round offices in Springfield, laying claim to some of the newest and most attractive office buildings within walking distance of the Capitol.

But the largest contingent of state representatives in Springfield are the employees of state government. Dozens of state agencies, commissions and offices are headquartered in Springfield. The city is also home to several state facilities, including

The grand facade of the Illinois Supreme Court, part of the Capitol Complex downtown.

the Southern Illinois University School of Medicine, Sangamon State University and the Andrew McFarland Mental Health Center. Several other state facilities, including five prisons, are within an easy commute. And so while much of state government activity in Springfield is seasonal, state employees constitute a year-round presence.

The sheer numbers of this population make them a formidable force in the local economy. With nearly 20,000 state employees living in Sangamon County, many families can claim at least one. In fact, a recent study showed that about 20 percent of all state workers in Sangamon County live in a household that includes at least one other state employee.

But many other factors combine to enhance the economic impact on this work force. Despite periodic shifts among the office holders, state government is a relatively stable employer. Springfield is home to hundreds of career public administrators who occupy top posts in state government, as well as to thousands who hold jobs through retirement—despite the vagaries of election years.

The presence of these career employees helps

Perhaps it's because the city's roots are so firmly planted in the business of government, but Springfieldians vote in numbers that far outstrip those found elsewhere in the United States.

POLLING PLACE

POLLS OPEN 6 A.M. CLOSE 7 P.M.

push the average salary for a state worker living in Sangamon County up to a highly respectable figure of $30,500 annually. Thus, as consumers and wage-earners, state employees play key roles in the stability of the local economy. In 1991, the unemployment rate in Sangamon County was just 4.8 percent, compared with 7.1 percent in Illinois and

Not all the public-sector activity in Springfield originates with the state. The new County Courts Complex symbolizes the strong presence of regional government.

The imposing modern Lincoln Library, in downtown Springfield.

6.7 percent nationally.

"Other forms of industry, particularly manufacturing, tend to foster more economic activity than a service economy such as Springfield's," said Richard J. Judd, professor of business administration at Sangamon State University in Springfield. "The blessing of a service economy is that it tends to moderate swings in the general economy. While Springfield may lag in the movement of cycles that cause boom or bust elsewhere in the nation, it also rides out the dips with much less trauma."

To take a closer look at this phenomenon, the Southern Illinois University medical school commissioned an economic-impact study in 1990. The report, prepared by a local market analysis group, found that the school's annual expenditure of $37 million in Sangamon County created an additional 3,295 jobs, which, taken together, created residential construction worth about $9 million and stimulated additional savings of $7 million and direct deposits of $12 million.

The study, however, also takes pains to point out that to measure the school's impact only in economic terms is to overlook some of its most important contributions to the local community.

"The presence of the S.I.U. School of Medicine creates a concentration of specialized services and advanced research in the two local affiliated hospitals that otherwise simply would not be possible," said Dr. Richard H. Moy, dean and provost of the medical school since its founding in 1970.

And so it is with the other state agencies, offices and institutions that occupy Springfield. Their very presence not only boosts the economy, it also provides business opportunities for others and a ready availability of specialized services and opportunities that enriches life in the community.

Many state services that generally can be obtained only by mail are available on a walk-in, same-day basis in Springfield. Taxes can be paid, licenses renewed and reports filed in a timely manner. There is also a generally high awareness among the local populace of services offered by state government. For example, special-order vanity and personalized license plates from the secretary of state's office are a common sight—and the general opinion seems to be WY NOT U 2?

Springfield residents also have ready access to many state records. While several state agencies have decentralized their operations with satellites around the state, Springfield remains the repository for the vast bulk of Illinois' records and artifacts.

Hundreds of thousands of visitors come to Springfield each year looking for clues to their past. Many genealogical researchers find key sources of information in the Illinois State Archives and the Illinois State Library. The library also keeps full-time researchers on staff who respond to public requests for information and oversee a huge interlibrary loan operation that provides books upon request to libraries throughout the state.

The Illinois State Historical Library, operated by the Illinois Historic Preservation Agency in a sub-basement of the Old State Capitol, maintains a large collection of Lincoln papers as well as tracts, books and other materials reflecting Illinois' history from early times to the present. In addition, the Illinois State Museum offers collections of geological materials, art and dioramas depicting the life of Illinois' plants, native animals and earliest dwellers.

Surrounded by and steeped in state government, it is perhaps natural that the denizens of Springfield also seem to take the whole process of government more seriously than people in many other communities. While nationally a majority of voting-age adults might choose to stay home on Election Day, more than 81 percent of Springfield's registered voters turned out for the last presidential election.

In these and many other ways, great and small, state government penetrates and shapes the life of the community.

LOCAL GOVERNMENT

Long before it became Illinois' capital city, Springfield was a government town. In the early days of statehood, Springfield snared the distinction of becoming a county seat, with the help, one account suggests, of a bit of skulduggery. Other locations in frontier Sangamon County may have offered more natural advantages as a government center, but the city fathers of the new settlement of Springfield showed exceptional aptitude for making the most of their opportunities.

As the story goes, the choices had narrowed to three towns in March of 1825, when a five-member state commission appointed by the legislature arrived to select a permanent site for the Sangamon County seat. The front-runner was a town called Sangamo, situated on a high bluff overlooking the Sangamon River, about seven miles northwest of Springfield.

But to Springfield's lasting benefit, the commissioners' guide on their selection tour was a Springfield man. He took the delegation first to Springfield, and seeing that they were not persuaded, led them on to Sangamo—by a highly inconvenient route. After traversing a creek, thickets, sloughs and almost impassable marshes, the commissioners caught their first sight of Sangamo. They agreed the town was well situated along the river, but was "most difficult to access," according to a 1904 history of Springfield. To clinch that impression, their guide took them back to Springfield over a different, but no less difficult, route. The exhausted commissioners named Springfield the county seat. Their guide, Elijah Iles, is memorialized in Springfield with a school, a park and a major thoroughfare.

The new distinction cemented Springfield's pre-eminence in the county. Recognized as a center for both trade and governmental transactions, the town continued to grow, and in 1832 it was incorporated. Sangamo, meanwhile, became a footnote in county history.

In modern-day Springfield and Sangamon County, local government remains an influential force for growth and development. With a work force of 9,000, local government in the greater Springfield region is also a major employer.

The city of Springfield, perhaps due to its long acquaintance with both state and local politics, operates a highly service-oriented government at a relatively low cost to residents.

The city's tax rate was lowered to $1 per $100 assessed valuation in 1984 and has stayed there since, largely due to the adoption of a 1 percent sales tax. With the city's continued growth and development as a regional retail center, booming sales-tax receipts finance a major share of city government operations. In 1992, that source of income accounted for slightly more than half of the city's $35 million corporate budget.

From 1922 until the late 1980s, Springfield operated under a mayor-commission form of government, with a mayor and elected commissioners dividing responsibility for the various departments of government. However, in a landmark decision in January 1987, a federal judge ruled that at-large elections for Springfield's commissioners effectively prevented black candidates from ever winning a seat on the council, a violation of the U.S. Voting Rights Act. Springfield was ordered to adopt a new form of government.

Following an advisory referendum that yielded no clear mandate, city officials met with reformers and negotiated a transitional government. Over a four-year period, Springfield phased out its elect-

Ready to serve: some of the firefighters of the new Toronto Road Firehouse.

ed commissioners, placing their departments under the control of a nonpartisan mayor and a council of ten aldermen by the spring of 1991. Ironically, Springfield's latest government reform was a return to a system that was widely vilified in 1911, when the city adopted the commission form of government, "a notable stride in the right direction," according to an editorial in the *Illinois State Register*.

Most city departments are now under the direct supervision of the mayor, who also wields a tiebreaking vote on the council. Operating out of a City Hall that now encompasses the former county building next door, the mayor directly oversees a host of city services, while aldermen hold sway over the budget and many policy questions.

Taken as a whole, city government has a major influence on the availability of services and quality of life in Springfield. Nowhere is this more apparent than in the operation of the municipal utility, City Water, Light & Power, which employs close to half of the city's work force of 1,650. Established in 1916, C.W.L.P. has grown to a $150 million-a-year operation, with 61,400 electric customers and a 500-mile-long water distribution system serving about 80 percent of Sangamon County's population. Both electric and water rates are well below nationwide averages, and C.W.L.P.'s Springfield customers pay the lowest residential electric rates in Illinois.

From its earliest days, C.W.L.P. has engineered many of the city's most ambitious undertakings,

including the construction of Lake Springfield in 1933, in the middle of the "Dust Bowl" drought. The 4,040-acre lake is the city's chief water supply, cools five lakeside power stations, and serves as a major recreation area. Public parks, boat ramps and a beach share the 57-mile shoreline with private houses and a yacht club that is home to the dozens of sailboats that dot the lake spring through fall.

Extremely low rainfalls in 1987 and 1988 led the city council to move ahead in 1989 with plans for a supplemental water supply. By late 1992, about 85 percent of the necessary acreage had been acquired for Hunter Lake, named for a former city commissioner. Construction is targeted to begin as early as 1995 and the lake should be serving the community by the end of the decade.

Springfield city government also takes an active role in providing other services. The quality of its fire department has given the city the best possible insurance rating, which translates to lower rates for customers. With landfills reaching capacity across the nation, the public works department has been creating programs to promote curbside recycling and waste reduction. The city-funded health department offers free immunization clinics, physical examinations for school children, AIDS counseling, a child nutrition program and a host of other services.

On the cultural side, the city oversees an International Visitors Bureau, a Convention and Visitors Bureau and the well-regarded Lincoln Library. Using an electronic indexing system, library patrons can make selections from about 365,000 volumes and other items, including periodicals, record albums, compact discs, videos and even a modest art collection. In addition, the library maintains a professional reference desk, children's sections, a large-print collection and the Sangamon Valley Collection, a treasure trove of area historical and genealogical information. The main library is in a three-story modern structure just north of the Lincoln Home National Historic Site, with branches operating on the city's West and Southeast sides.

Other governmental units play their distinctive roles in enhancing Springfield life. The mass transit district operates a fleet of 64 vehicles, including 22 equipped for handicap access, on a six-day-a-week schedule. The Prairie Capital Convention Center oversees a 40,000-square-foot

Today's environmental issues allow even the youngest of citizens to contribute to the commonwealth by taking part in recycling efforts.

facility, capable of seating 8,000, that sees an eclectic mix of events, including rock concerts, tractor pulls, sports events and other shows.

Rounding out the local public service sector is the county government, overseen by a board of 29 elected members who choose a chairperson. In late 1991, county government moved into a new seven-story complex, topped with dramatic arches and equipped with state-of-the-art courtrooms and a 290-bed jail. Under the supervision of nine elected administrators, the county collects real estate taxes, operates a busy court system, administers a "911" emergency telephone system, polices rural Sangamon County, oversees land-use planning and maintains 270 miles of highways and 63 bridges.

FEDERAL GOVERNMENT

A plot of federal land encompassing four blocks near downtown Springfield is a magnet for visitors from around the world. In it lies the home of a man one Springfield observer described as "the most durable ghost in American life," Abraham Lincoln. The only house Lincoln ever owned is now operated as an historic site by the National Park Service—the crowning jewel of the Lincoln sites in Springfield. Reopened in 1988 following a $2.2 million renovation, the two-story frame house has been meticulously returned to its Lincoln-era appearance. Its earthy exterior colors are identical to those on the house when the Lincolns were in residence, and the wallpaper in Lincoln's bedroom has been reproduced down to the last color-colliding flourish. Work on the site has continued, with restoration of the homes neighboring the Lincoln's, which have recently been made available for lease by other federal agencies.

"One of the greatest charms of the Lincoln Home area is the fact that visitors can almost step back in time, down a wooden sidewalk, and see Lincoln's neighborhood much as he saw it," said U.S. Representative Richard J. Durbin, whose district office became the historic site's first tenant, in 1989. "Creating opportunities for the other houses to be occupied only promotes upkeep of the site and increases the vitality of the whole neighborhood."

While the Lincoln site is by far the federal government's most widely known installation in Springfield, it is far from the largest. That distinction goes to the National Guard, which last year secured nearly $47 million in federal funding to maintain Army units at Camp Lincoln and the 183rd Tactical Fighter Group at Springfield's Capital Airport. Together, the two divisions received nearly a third of the federal government's total spending for Guard units in Illinois.

The Guard's chief mission is to provide a combat-ready force of "citizen soldiers" who can be mobilized in times of war and national emergency. But the units also have a state role. They stand prepared to provide disaster relief, assist in civil defense and maintain public order. In addition both the Army and Air National Guard units play a major role in the local community, sponsoring fund-raisers, scouting functions and club and church activities.

"Besides our community involvement, and equally important, our existence creates secondary jobs and produces a positive economic impact on central Illinois," said Col. Richard E. McLane II, commander of the 183rd Tactical Fighter Group at Capital Airport. With a force of 24 single-seat F-16s, the Air Guard unit maintains close to 1,200 military and 300 civilian personnel. In addition, McLane said, the unit estimates that its activity creates more than 370 secondary jobs, producing a total economic impact of about $43 million on the region.

Other federal installations in Springfield include a regional post office, a U.S. District Courthouse and a district office for the Internal Revenue Service that conducts audits and collections for the southern two-thirds of Illinois. Most federal offices, including those of four different agricultural agencies, are scattered throughout town. The General Services Administration, headed in the early 1990s by the former Sangamon County Board chairman, is considering a proposal to build a new federal building to house 30 government agencies and their 1,333 employees in a single location.

Top: Two members of the Air National Guard prepare their aircraft for a maneuver.

Bottom: Springfield is uncommonly well-supplied with governmental and quasi-governmental services on all levels. Here, the new state-of-the-art post office.

5

Vital Links

"IN THE EARLIER DAYS of Springfield, ere her limits had been extended," reminisced the historian John Carroll Power in 1872, "the educational facilities were not of the most magnificent description. No palatial school houses then reared their stately fronts within our limits, no school board supervised the movements of the educators of youth, and no army of teachers, patient, toiling instructors of the youthful mind, were to be found within the boundaries of the city."

Though inclined to the kind of overblown phrases popular in the Victorian era, Power essentially got it right: education in Springfield before the Civil War was a haphazard thing at best. But Springfield citizens had founded a prospering town where, by all economic and transportation good sense, none should exist—and had gained for that town the twin honors of being named county seat and then state capital. These were not the sort of people to let Springfield's educational advantages

The newest laboratory techniques are put into action in Springfield's oldest hospital, St. John's, which opened in 1875 and has been growing ever since.

At Dubois Elementary School, students receive the training that befits their status as Springfield's leaders of the twenty-first century.

It's all smiles at one of Springfield's well-equipped public-school playgrounds.

lag behind those of other cities in the state.

By an amended city charter, approved March 2, 1854, the Springfield Public Schools were born, offering free education to all citizens, many of whom would otherwise have been unable to afford instruction for their children in the few private city schools of the day. By the time of Power's reminiscence, Springfield had a high school and full complement of elementary schools. To use his words, the era of the "palatial" school house had arrived: "In the list of advantages possessed by Springfield, none is greater than that of her institutions of learning, her temples of instruction and her seats of popular and general education.... Our city government has sought, by extending a liberal hand, to foster and promote within our midst the glorious and beneficent scheme of popular education."

In short, Springfield had achieved a first-class educational system in less than one generation. Despite economic ups and downs, local citizens have continued to do their best in promoting a high level of public and private schooling. District 186, as the Springfield schools were eventually numbered, boasts three high schools—Springfield, Lanphier and Southeast; three middle schools—Franklin, Grant and Washington—and 26 elementary schools. The district also operates the Lawrence Adult Education Center. A variety of

programs are available for the handicapped, aged three to 21, in the district's comprehensive Special Education Department. Students may receive placement in Hearing Impaired, Learning Disabled, Speech and Language Impaired, Emotionally Disturbed, and Health Impairments programs.

The regular curriculum, in the words of a recently issued guide, "emphasizes reading, spelling, composition, handwriting, mathematics, social studies and science. In addition, health, art, music and physical education instruction is provided all students either by a specialist or by a classroom teacher." This curriculum is reviewed annually. Reading groups, programmed learning and a range of enrichment activities like the Young Authors event complement basic instruction. District 186's Gifted Program integrates gifted students into regular classrooms as much as possible.

Every school in the district has a parent organization in which parents or guardians are encouraged to take active roles in their children's education. Dozens of citizens offer their time and labor in the School Volunteer Program. In Springfield, national concerns over declining quality in education are being met head-on. With a 1993 enrollment of more than 15,800 students, the district encompasses 65 square miles and includes the entire city, adjoining villages and some surrounding unincorporated areas. Continued, rapid expansion appears to be the trend during the remaining years of the 1990s, with predicted enrollment reaching around 18,000 students by the decade's end.

With a staff of over 1,400 and an annual budget approaching $5 million, District 186 also exerts a major economic impact in central Illinois. A *State Journal-Register* story of September 1991 gave a fascinating glimpse into the facts and figures of the Springfield schools—everything from the number of bars of soap used annually (56,000) to the number of computers owned (750).

More seriously, the survey outlines an impressive and complex institution that serves populations of socially, culturally, economically and ethnically diverse students. For example, it says, "More than a quarter of District 186's student population are members of minority groups. The vast majority of those students are black." But Asian, Native American and Hispanic populations continue to grow. Still, statistics cannot show some things—like the experience and dedication of a teaching staff (average age: 42.5 years old) working to educate and motivate this wide-ranging population.

In 1977, at a time when the District was experiencing acute financial distress, the School Board hired Dr. Donald Miedema as superintendent.

Miedema directly told a concerned board that he wanted to stay for 10 years in order to reach some of his goals for the district. Many were skeptical, remembering that most superintendents in recent times had lasted no more than four years. Fourteen years later, in June of 1991, Miedema retired as superintendent and recalled for *State Journal-Register* writer Diana Penner the many changes that had taken place during his tenure. Not the least among them were a hotly contested bond issue in 1984, which set the district on firmer financial footing, and the resulting physical improvements to school facilities.

Robert Hill was a young school administrator who had learned his trade under Miedema and was eventually named deputy superintendent. So pleased were School Board members with Hill's attributes that even after a nationwide search, they appointed him to replace his former boss. This move received wide community support. Hill's management style is praised by business leaders and fellow educators, many from the city's private schools, like Sister Marilyn Jean Runkel, associate director for elementary education of the Roman Catholic Diocese. She complimented Hill for routinely going "beyond what is required by law to ensure that parochial students are fairly served."

This cooperative spirit—as well as the more common friendly rivalry between the private and public schools—is an important aspect of Springfield education, leading to high achievement by both spheres. The city has long offered a broad range of choices in private education. The Ursuline nuns established a convent school in 1855, only a year after public education began in the city. That school still operates as the Ursuline Academy high school, joining the recently merged Sacred Heart and Griffin high schools as part of a system of education that includes nine elementary schools attached to numerous parishes throughout the city and comprises the largest segment of non-public school enrollment in Springfield.

The Lutheran Church maintains four parochial grade schools and one high school. Local Baptist and Christian churches run Calvary Academy, offering a nondenominational elementary and high school education. Three Montessori programs, numerous preschools and even some home education programs add variety to the traditional public and parochial picture. Nonpublic enrollment currently stands at around 6,000 students.

BUSINESS AND VOCATIONAL EDUCATION

Educational opportunities abound for post high school students as well. Business and vocational instruction play a vital part in local educa-

tion. Springfield is a business community and offers careers to those prepared with the proper skills. Brown's Business College grants diplomas in secretarial skills, word processing, accounting and court reporting, for which there is great local demand. Brown's aggressive marketing has resulted in increased enrollment and construction of a new facility, which opened in late 1988. The school has been a part of Springfield since 1864, when it was opened as the Rutledge Davison Business College by Washington Rutledge, a relative of Abraham Lincoln's reputed love, Ann Rutledge. Though far newer to Springfield, Robert Morris College is a branch of a long-established school and offers degrees in allied health, secretarial and business administration programs in a newly constructed complex on the city's Southwest Side.

Nor is vocational education ignored. Springfield's Capital Area Vocational Center opened in the late 1960s under the auspices of the Springfield School District. From a small rented building, the program moved to the former Feitshans High School on South 15th Street and eventually to its own large building near Lake Springfield. Beginning with a few students interested in automobile mechanics, the program proved phenomenally successful. Today, students can choose from courses in building trades, electronics, plumbing, data processing, commercial cooking and an enlarged mechanical and body automobile repair program among other subjects. C.A.V.C. students have built several houses, thus contributing in a very real way to the growth of Springfield. The school is a far cry from its early days when, as the current director, Kent Siders, recalls, it was a place a few "car-crazy students could go to learn a little bit about mechanics."

COLLEGES AND UNIVERSITIES

Except for the now-closed Concordia Theological Seminary and Lincoln College of Law (both single-purpose schools), Springfield College in Illinois was, for 40 years, the sole institution of higher education in Springfield. Founded in 1929 by the

Learning can take place in many settings. An old-time carpenter demonstrates his honored craft at the Clayville Rural Life Center and Museum, in the nearby town of Clayville.

Ursuline nuns, Springfield Junior College (as it was originally known) adjoins Ursuline High School and includes the beautiful and historic George M. Brinkerhoff mansion as part of its tree-shaded North Side campus. The college's relative smallness has allowed for high-quality, personalized instruction with a faculty-student ratio of 1 to 12. The music department is only one outstanding program to choose from in the school's liberal arts curriculum. S.C.I.'s tradition has been one of high quality education for highly motivated students. Recent research showed that a very large percentage of the practicing attorneys, physicians, dentists and veterinarians in Springfield began their careers at S.C.I. And 98 percent of S.C.I. graduates are accepted for admission to their first choice colleges or universities. This comes as no surprise from a place rated "one of the five best junior colleges in Illinois" by the Illinois Community College Board. When a suggestion was made recently that the college be closed and that the students' needs could be met elsewhere, students, faculty and hundreds of alumni rallied and vocalized their opposition to the plan. Their loyalty is a clear sign that they are pleased with the school's high quality of education and of their commitment to keeping it available for future generations.

When the first members of the baby-boom generation reached college age, in the 1960s, college and university classrooms across the country were suddenly filled to overflowing. Springfield community leaders recognized an opportunity to fill some of that need by bringing three new institutions of higher learning to the city. In 1966, representatives from 25 area high-school districts gathered and determined a need for a public community college in the Springfield area. Members of this group drafted a feasibility study report which led to the establishment of the Lincoln Land Junior College District. In a referendum approved by voters on February 23, 1967, Lincoln Land Junior College, under President Dr. Robert L. Poorman, opened to an enrollment of more than 1,450 students in six temporary barracks-like structures, earning it the affectionate nickname of Plywood U. The original junior college name was changed to community college in 1968 to better reflect the school's broad community appeal with "attention to day and evening programs for students wishing occupational training and transfer and continuing education." The college quickly stepped through its paces to gain full accreditation. In 1968, the first acreage for a permanent campus was acquired and in 1974 it was opened to students. L.L.C.C. then boasted a large library building overlooking the campus lake, a gymnasium, multipurpose building

Above: Springfield College in Illinois, founded in 1929, was for 40 years the only institution of higher learning in the city.

Left: A rare quiet moment at Lincoln Land Community College. An Illinois State University study of the 1980s showed students from this institution ranking first academically among transfer students from community colleges.

and generous classroom space. Most campus structures incorporated advanced energy-saving technology and design, including solar collection prisms and even a wind-powered generator. L.L.C.C.'s generous academic program included more than 250 course offerings in 37 fields, with more than half of the courses in vocational and technical fields like agriculture, drafting, electronics, health and technical and secretarial sciences. Programs in nursing, automotive technology, law enforcement and radiology technology fill important needs in Springfield's service, medical and manufacturing sectors by turning out skilled workers in those fields.

Students can receive instruction off campus as well, in 30 communities throughout the college district and various non-campus Springfield sites. L.L.C.C. also sponsors Springfield's Community Volunteer Center, which provides service to more than 125 not-for-profit agencies in the area, a Fire Science Training Program, a Displaced Homemak-

Opposite: In the library of Sangamon State University, founded in 1970 as a unique "public affairs university." With the entire state capital as its laboratory and classroom, it is a distinguished institution that forges links between the worlds of academia and public policy.

ers Program and a Business-Industry Development Center. The college and community have developed a finely tuned partnership of achievement.

After a long, successful tenure as president, Dr. Robert Poorman retired in 1988 and was replaced by Dr. William D. Law, Jr., whose philosophy of college-community cooperation is in keeping with Lincoln Land's traditions. The college's "outstanding and well-recognized record in

Above: The Springfield Clinic, today a pillar of Springfield's burgeoning medical community, was founded in 1939 when five doctors combined their practices.

Right: The Cardiac Rehabilitation Unit at Memorial Medical Center focuses on wellness rather than on sickness.

preparing students to move on to four-year colleges remains among the very best in the state of Illinois," says Bill Law, as he is familiarly known throughout the college district. "Similarly, those students who come to prepare to enter the work force continue to find that their education at Lincoln Land Community College opens doors for them in business and industry." "Nowhere," he insists, will be found a "board of trustees, faculty and staff more devoted and committed to assuring that each student's experience will be the very best it can be." As a testimony to the college's success, an Illinois State University study in the 1980s showed that L.L.C.C. students ranked first academically among those from community colleges, with more than 100 students transferring to Illinois State.

Many graduates of Springfield College in Illinois and Lincoln Land Community College continue their education in Springfield at Sangamon State University. S.S.U. is one of the two upper-level universities founded in Illinois in the wake of the Illinois Master Plan developed by the Illinois Board of Higher Education in the mid-1960s. The Illinois Legislature authorized planning for the school in 1967 and appropriated operating funds

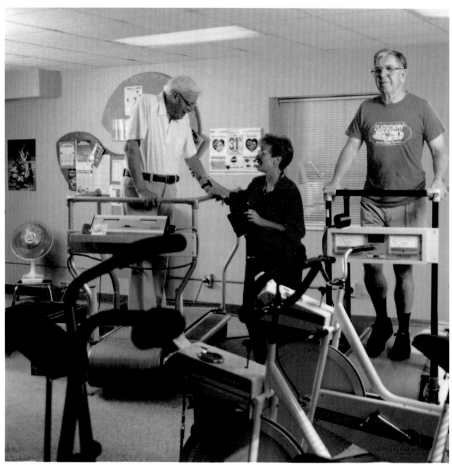

in 1969. In September 1970, just three years after initial planning, the University, still housed in interim quarters, opened with more than 800 students and 45 faculty members. The first students were graduated even before the first president, Dr. Robert Spencer, was officially installed. S.S.U. was designated as the state's public affairs university, which is particularly appropriate given its location in the state capital. This public affairs commitment, in the words of an early school catalog, means involvement with "training persons for public service and, more basically, with fostering an active understanding of contemporary social, environmental, technological and ethical problems as they relate to public policy." In the 1990s, nearly a generation after its founding, the university operates with a commitment to the same philosophy of addressing "public affairs within the framework of a liberal arts curriculum" with an emphasis on "practical experience, professional development and innovative teaching."

The school has grown physically with its move to a permanent campus of over 600 acres located near Lake Springfield and adjoining Lincoln Land Community College. Sangamon State University has a current enrollment of approximately 4,000 students and has 180 faculty members. The school has expanded academically as well, presently having more than 40 degree programs from which to choose. The university's first president, Dr. Robert Spencer, guided the school through its heady first days, which were filled with the excitement of students and faculty making history in a totally new institution. President Spencer is fondly remembered in the Springfield community for his personal commitment to excellence. In retirement, he recalled some high points in his event-filled life. "Professor, [college] president, senator and Christian thinker" are just some of the achievements mentioned in one biographical sketch. His life's journey has included a commitment to serving others—and this is the philosophy he wove into the fabric of S.S.U. Spencer's dedication to public service led him to work in Catholic Worker bread lines and soup kitchens in Brooklyn during World War II. He brought this same desire to serve others with him to the Vermont statehouse when he was elected a state senator. Spencer summed up his ideas on running a university like S.S.U.: "Basically, the university

community is one that runs on the professional respect for other people's judgment and decisions, and a tolerance for the diversity of views." Sangamon State University has been a model of that ideal.

From its first days, S.S.U. has maintained its commitment to the students and to providing a quality education while recognizing the importance of public service. Each student is required to spend an Applied Studies Term working in the community. Quality in teaching extends even to the university's Orris L. Brookens Library, where instruction in the use of library sources by library faculty on a one-to-one basis is an ongoing practice. And the entire city is used as laboratory and campus for academic study.

Programs "are structured to make use of the capital city's resources, particularly state and federal agencies that provide internship, experiential and research opportunities," says the school's official materials. "Students have access to the deliberations of the General Assembly.... Legislators and other elected officials, lobbyists, agency heads and commissioners are a vital part of the Springfield scene and comprise an incomparable human resource. Politics in all forms can be studied in Springfield, from the day-to-day functioning of regulatory commissions, legislative committees or local government bodies to groups of demonstrators on the statehouse lawn."

The university's Institute for Public Affairs consists of the Center for Legal Studies, Illinois Legislative Studies Center, the WSSU public radio station (a National Public Radio affiliate), a television office and *Illinois Issues* magazine. The Sangamon State University Auditorium, housed in the Public Affairs Center, is a 2,000-plus-seat theater that hosts more than 60 music, theater and dance performances a year. As S.S.U. heads toward its quarter-century mark, the school has become an integral part of Springfield

> T wenty years after its founding, S.I.U. Medical School successes are legion.

Doctor's Hospital, which opened in 1975, is a relative newcomer among Springfield's medical institutions.

and reflects its political, social and cultural life.

At around the same time that S.S.U. came into being, another university was being planned for Springfield, making the 1960s the most productive and exciting decade for education to date, and bringing incredible opportunities for study, research and a host of related activities. Despite the fact that Illinois had four medical schools in Chicago in the 1960s, the majority of the graduates were leaving the state to practice elsewhere. Facing this discouraging statistic, the Illinois Board of Higher Education decided on a bold move to found a completely new downstate medical school.

The Southern Illinois University School of Medicine came into existence in January 1970 when Dr. Richard H. Moy was made dean—even before there were students, faculty, buildings, campus or curriculum. The major interest of the new university developed quickly: providing doctors for small communities and rural areas of the state, particularly in prenatal and obstetric care. School officials signed an affiliation agreement with

total education, S.I.U. developed a teaching theater-museum around the theme of the Development of Primary Care Healing in the Upper Mississippi River Basin. This theater is a unique facility for the teaching of medical humanities and was funded with a combination of state, federal and private monies. A complete nineteenth-century doctor's office and pharmacy, donated by Dr. Emmet Pearson, are two outstanding components of the facility that are also used for general public education. S.I.U.-MED library is also an important cultural addition to Springfield. Here, trained biomedical librarians assist users in searching its vast collection of books, journals, audio-visual and on-line reference sources. A special collections room features well over 1,000 historical medical books and journals.

Twenty years after its founding, the school's successes are legion. A 1987 survey by *U.S. News & World Report* of medical school deans around the country named S.I.U. Medical School the institution most commonly cited for innovation.

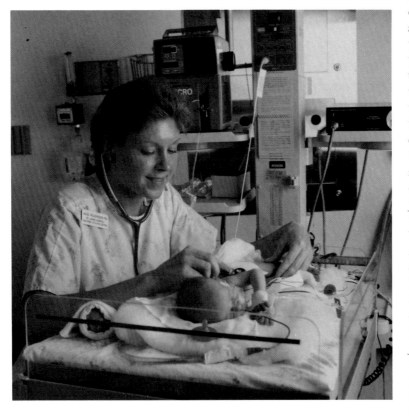

St. John's Hospital's tradition of high-quality neonatal care, especially for high-risk babies, goes back to 1916.

Springfield's St. John's Hospital and Memorial Medical Center and S.I.U.-MED truly became a teaching university with a "competency-based" system. This means that students must perform at a required level and not merely rely on passing grades in order to graduate.

Recognizing the need for doctors to receive a

An annual Doctors' Fair gives officials from Illinois towns and rural areas a chance to promote their communities to prospective graduates. And the school has made astounding physical growth as well, resulting in more than a ripple in the local economy. A 1990 economic impact study by Health Market Analysis, Inc., showed that the school had directly created nearly 700 jobs and had led indirectly to the creation of 5,400 more. Total purchasing power generated by the medical school is estimated to be over $300 million annually. Summing up the S.I.U. success story, pharmacology professor Donald Caspary told Springfield's *State Journal-Register*, "I have to go like *this* to believe it," he said, pinching his arm. "It's an amazing story. You could go to Munich, you could go to St. Louis, you could go to Austin, Texas—and they would have heard of little old S.I.U."

SPRINGFIELD'S MEDICAL COMMUNITY

It was no accident that an institution like the S.I.U. School of Medicine chose to locate in Springfield, which has been described as "downstate Illinois' largest medical center,"—no small compliment in a state that includes several other, larger, cities like Peoria, Rockford and the Moline area. Three hospitals, a major clinic, 20 nursing homes, 300 doctors and thousands of medical workers make up a comprehensive health care community in Greater Springfield.

The oldest hospital, St. John's, opened in one small building in 1875, and developed into the major regional hospital of today. The first Catholic school of nursing was founded there in 1886 and still operates. Schools of anesthesia and medical technology followed. The forerunner of today's High-Risk Neonatal Center opened at the hospital in 1916. A $30 million rebuilding program in the mid-1970s allowed development of the Regional Trauma Center, Cancer Treatment Center, the first central Illinois Poison Control Resource Center and a Hospice and Chemical Dependence center. The hospital, with its 800-plus bed capacity, was the first of 12 Illinois and Wisconsin hospitals opened and maintained by the Hospital Sisters of the Third Order of St. Francis under the Hospital Sisters Health System.

Memorial Medical Center, Southern Illinois University Medical School's other affiliate hospital, opened in 1897 as Springfield Hospital under the auspices of the Lutheran Church. It became Memorial Hospital in 1941 with construction of the first part of the present complex at First and Miller streets. In 1974, the name changed again, to Memorial Medical Center, to better reflect the many new diagnostic, clinical and technical services offered. An outstanding burn unit, the first Midwestern laboratory designed to research and diagnose inner-ear and eye disfunctions and a well-known Regional Cancer Program are only a few of these services. Together, St. John's and Memorial provide a unique laboratory in which S.I.U. faculty, staff and area medical students can learn to become skilled health care providers.

Doctors Hospital, the latest entry in the field, opened its doors in August 1975. This 200-patient private hospital was designed to provide space for the rapidly expanding, but sometimes overcrowded, Memorial and St. John's facilities. Full hospital services, including surgery, were offered to patients from the first day. In 1988, 60 local individuals purchased the entire operation. The medical and support staff have worked diligently to promote acceptance of this latest addition to Springfield's

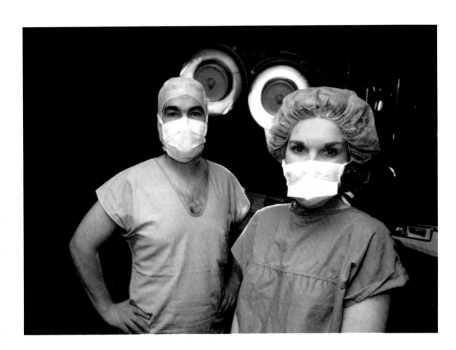

medical facilities.

The Springfield Clinic was another newcomer to medicine in Springfield in November 1939 when five Springfield doctors joined their practices to form this new enterprise. The individual doctors developed specialties and gradually expanded throughout the 1940s, '50s and '60s until the clinic became an important regional health care provider. Today, patients receive care in 17 fields—everything from obstetrics to orthopedics, cardiology to dermatology, and even family practice. The clinic, in the words of one book, is "a team of physicians and dentists who have pooled their resources and knowledge in their respective fields to provide the highest standard of health care for Springfield and the central Illinois area."

The combination of diverse educational opportunities and a first-class health care system is a major factor in Springfield's continued growth and economic good health as well as an important reason for justifiable civic pride. Families relocating to Springfield are often pleased to discover this combination, a part of the whole which makes Springfield truly one of the livable cities in the country.

Even with masks, confidence and dedication are evident in this operating-room team.

6

Heart and Soul

DESCRIBED IN A RECENT survey as the nation's "fourth most perfectly ordinary town," Springfield in many ways offers a slice of life in the U.S.A. Which is not to say that Illinois' capital is merely *only* typical.

Springfield has any number of attributes that make it uniquely Springfield—pink cabs and tow trucks, an annual Fourth of July street party called LincolnFest and an open-faced cheese-drenched sandwich known as the horseshoe whose origins are still a topic of heated debate. More important, Springfield's all-time most illustrious resident, Abraham Lincoln, is an American icon. But the millions of visitors who come from all over the world to walk in Lincoln's footsteps find more than hallowed relics of a great American's life in the 1850s. They find a city that is as vibrant and colorful as its past, with entertainments as diverse and utterly American as its populace.

From early-morning jogs through misty Washington Park to sunbaked afternoons

One of Springfield's favorite sporting events is called Abe's Amble. Some amble! It's a breakneck 10-kilometer race.

Opposite: Every year, the scouts' pilgrimage to Lincoln's Tomb illustrates the monument's importance as a national shrine.

Top: The Dana-Thomas House by Frank Lloyd Wright (1902) is one of the nation's architectural treasures.

Bottom: White becomes its own palette when snow season comes to Springfield's parks.

at the Illinois State Fair and cool late nights at a local blues club, Springfield offers a smorgasbord of recreational opportunities that span both the clock and the calendar. Whether one's idea of fun turns to inspiration or perspiration, the city and its environs offer plenty to enjoy.

In many ways, life in Springfield finds a middle ground between the sophistication and diversity of a major city and the informality and warmth of a small town. The city supports a thriving arts community as well as countless softball leagues. Residents can attend lectures by nationally known figures or browse among the 4-H Club entries at the Sangamon County Fair. They can dine at restaurants offering the latest innovations in cuisine or savor a tamale smothered in chili at a local tavern. Springfield has the soul and aspirations of a major city, but at its heart is a load of small-town charm.

The community's interest in the arts and recreation is a long-standing tradition, harking back to its days as a bustling prairie settlement. One suspiciously apocryphal tale suggests that the area's legislators may even have won votes for Springfield as state capital by suggesting that it was capable of providing lawmakers with more comfortable amenities than the city of Vandalia. This means that rather than sating the legislative appetite with the usual assortment of wild game, Springfield would also provide hog meat. But even more refining influences were in store. As early as the 1840s, the state's brand-new capital city "assumed an air of gaiety and intellectual rapport," wrote one of the divas of Springfield's nineteenth-century social set. "There were parties, cotillions, balls, concerts and lectures to keep us entertained."

Needless to say, the city's chief amusements have changed over the years. But interest in promoting the entertainment and enlightenment of the citizenry has continued unabated. Now, after more than 150 years as the capital city, Springfield has expanded its menu of possibilities far beyond hog meat.

The prairie capital boasts a vital, innovative arts community, with a municipal opera, a symphony, several theater groups, a ballet company and an active arts association. Many of these institutions have their roots in private funding and initiative. But no one source can take credit for the lively state of entertainment in Springfield, which partly explains the great diversity of offerings.

Some of the community's healthiest recreational institutions enjoy government support. Springfield has historically elected city leaders who look upon providing recreation as a civic duty. In 1900, voters elected seven trustees to the

Pleasure Driveway and Park District. Shortly thereafter, the trustees, all prominent Springfield businessmen, spent $4,250 to acquire a 17-acre, privately run pleasure ground, already known as Washington Park. It was the first acquisition for a spacious park system that has grown to include 30 parks, three popular golf courses, the Henson Robinson Zoo, the Thomas Rees Memorial Caril-

Springfieldians have always taken to aviation, and love an air-show display of historical planes.

lon, a botanical garden, indoor and outdoor pools and an ice skating rink.

In 1924, Springfield voters also gave their city government authority to collect taxes for recreational activities. The Springfield Recreation Department provides recreational programming throughout the city, including softball, volleyball, basketball and track. It also operates several city facilities, including velvety Lincoln Greens golf course along the shoreline of Lake Springfield, and Lanphier Park, the stadium that houses the city's Class A minor league baseball team.

State government, so omnipresent in Springfield life, also registers an impact on the local entertainment scene. The crowning event of the summer is the Illinois State Fair, held since 1853 to showcase the state's agricultural riches. The event unfolds each August on a 366-acre fairground at the city's North End, prompting a boomlet in parking services as landowners for blocks around transform normally tidy front lawns and vacant lots into impromptu parking lots. The festivities begin with the Twilight Parade and progress with nightly appearances by nationally known performers, harness racing with pari-mutuel betting, judging of all manner of livestock,

a carnival with up-to-the-minute thrills and spills, and beauty queens. Springfield residents turn out faithfully each year to partake of the familiar sights, including the traditional "butter cow" hand-sculpted each year from dozens of pounds of butter, and the "hawg trough," a display of prize specimens from Illinois waterways at Conservation World.

Illinois government is also the overseer of some of the area's most popular tourist destinations, including the meticulously restored Dana-Thomas House, the second most visited Frank Lloyd Wright house in the nation, and Lincoln's New Salem, a park comprising the historic restored village where the nation's 16th president grew to be "a man of purpose and destiny."

In addition, the state is a mostly silent partner in an organization that has been highly successful in promoting and advancing the celebration of the arts in three area counties. Formed in 1976, in the midst of efforts to mark the nation's 200th birthday, the Springfield Area Arts Council steers state funding to myriad local arts groups. It also oversees some of the community's most popular arts events, including First Night Springfield, the annual Children's Arts Festival, noontime concerts on the Old State Capitol Plaza and resident-artist programs in local schools.

Government and private organizations alike get into the act in sponsoring some of the area's most lively annual events, including the Old State Capitol Art Fair, the International Carillon Festival, the Illinois Central Blues Festival, the Ethnic Festival, Air Rendezvous, the Fine Crafts Fair, Maple Syrup Time, and the Traditional Music and Bluegrass Festival.

Springfield, once named by *Look* magazine as one of its All-American Cities, can still lay claim to a uniquely American flavor in the way its residents go about their daily lives. For many Springfield residents, enjoying life is a way of life.

SPRINGFIELD AT PLAY

Few people—apart from farmers—tend to think of the central Illinois landscape as a natural paradise. But along the banks of the Sangamon River the flat prairie succumbs to the gently rolling hills that characterize much of Springfield. The preservation of natural areas and creation of a variety of outdoor facilities give the region a wide choice of outdoor recreational activities. Here is a sampler:

PUBLIC PARKS AND RECREATION

The parks and open-space movement of the early 20th century gave Springfield the impetus to create a network of green spaces throughout the city. With a lineup of 32 parks comprising more than 2,400 acres, most residents have a park with playground equipment close by, with sports facilities also close at hand. But special features of the city's three major parks make them worth going the distance.

Springfield's oldest and most popular park is a 150-acre oasis of greenery and wildlife just minutes away from the state Capitol. Surrounded by some of the city's most pleasant and gracefully aging neighborhoods, Washington Park was originally a private development established by a Springfield streetcar company as a gimmick to attract patrons to the end of the line.

The park owes its natural state and winding network of roads to the landscape architect O. C. Simonds, best known for designing the Morton Arboretum near Chicago and Frick Park in Pittsburgh. Its central lagoon has become home to hundreds of ducks and geese who flock to the crusts and popcorn tossed out nightly by visitors.

Washington Park is home to the Springfield Park District's Botanical Garden, which boasts a 50-foot-diameter dome housing exotic tropical foliage and hundreds of flowering plants. Surrounding the conservatory are several colorful outdoor gardens, including a collection of 3,500 rose bushes brought to the peak of perfection for the annual Rose Walk in June. Nearby is a scent garden, with markers in Braille for the convenience of vision-impaired visitors, an iris and daylily garden featuring hundreds of varieties, and a glorious collection of chrysanthemums.

Within a short walk is the Thomas Rees Memorial Carillon, the site of an annual summer festival that draws carilloneurs from around the world. The 132-foot concrete tower, erected on the park's highest point, rings with bell-music performances throughout the summer.

While nearly half the size of Washington Park, 86-year-old Lincoln Park contains the most athletic facilities of any Springfield park. Most notably, it is the home of the Nelson Recreation Center, which offers an indoor ice rink and a large outdoor swimming pool. Lincoln Park also has several baseball diamonds, horseshoe pits, shuffleboard courts, tennis courts, a popular collection of playground equipment and a hiking trail.

For a glimpse of central Illinois as the Native Americans saw it, few things can touch the 340 acres of mostly undeveloped land in Carpenter Park. This dedicated nature preserve offers few sightings of humans, but pileated woodpeckers and native plants like columbine and purple trillium can be found in abundance.

The park district also operates the Henson Robinson Zoo. Dedicated in 1970 by the late Marlin Perkins, this picturesque zoological park near Lake Springfield is a place where people can hap-

Man-made Lake Springfield, which dates from the 1930s, is a source of both water and recreation. Its 57-mile shoreline is home to a yacht club, a marina and several free boat-launching facilities.

Springfield Recreation Department, along with a golf course and two ballparks, including the stadium where the Springfield Cardinals play.

The department operates the city's only true "urban" park, Union Square Park. Developed from a grant, the one-block downtown area includes a multitude of Victorian-design park benches, shuffleboard courts, horseshoe pits and a small playground.

At the opposite end of the park spectrum is the city's Riverside Park, a 700-acre tract along the Sangamon River that offers rural pleasures like camping, horseback riding, hay rides and housing for a B.M.X. club.

The department's main charge is creating recreational opportunities for people throughout the city. In that capacity, it oversees dozens of intramural leagues and events for special populations. Springfield has hosted the Illinois Senior Olympics since 1977 and is a qualifying site for the national games. The city established a Special Olympics program in 1979, and now serves about 400 mentally and physically challenged athletes each year.

WATERY DEEPS

While the central Illinois topography may seem best suited to acres of corn and soybeans, earth-moving equipment and engineering know-how also have invested it with acreage of the watery variety. Many of the Springfield area's lakes were built for practical reasons. They serve as public water supplies and cooling ponds for power plants. But they also provide lovely settings for a wide variety of leisure activities.

Lake Springfield's 4,235 acres are a regional playground, offering opportunities for fishing, boating, swimming, picnicking, hiking and bird watching. Its 57-mile shoreline is home to several free boat-launch facilities as well as the Island Bay Yacht Club and the Lake Springfield Marina, a six-acre amusement facility with a sand beach and rental jet skis. Eight public parks around the lake offer picnic tables and shelters, softball diamonds and playgrounds.

The city-operated Lake Beach, a sandy stretch with a vintage fieldstone beach house, is open for swimming throughout the summer. The beach offers periodic free swimming days and is accessible to persons with disabilities.

Although less developed, Sangchris Lake State Park offers a more pristine experience for nature lovers. The 2,162-acre lake, about 20 miles southeast of Springfield, is surrounded by about 1,400 acres of parkland donated by one of the state's major electrical utilities. Sangchris has camping,

Top: Folk-dancing clubs are places for Springfield's residents to keep their ethnic traditions alive, and enjoyably so.

Bottom: Dancers of the Springfield Ballet exercise in front of their most critical audience—themselves.

pily lose themselves among more than 300 exotic and domestic animals.

Listed among the nation's 160 accredited zoos, Henson Robinson has recently benefited from fresh leadership and a new influx of funding from another recreational activity in Springfield, the city's share of offtrack betting revenues.

The zoo recently added cheetahs, red wolves and a cougar exhibit, and is planning an Illinois wetlands area to house injured birds that cannot be released into the wild. The 14-acre zoo is also home to penguins, otter, lemurs and monkeys.

The city's two other parks are operated by the

picnicking and hiking facilities, but its main attractions are the largemouth bass, bluegill, crappie and catfish inhabiting its waters.

NATURE WALKS

The Adams Wildlife Sanctuary, tucked into a Springfield neighborhood, is an oasis of 30 acres of woodland and prairie managed by the Illinois Audubon Society. The sanctuary is a bird-watcher's delight, but its mile-long trail also offers sightings of small mammals, wildflowers and a striking three-acre prairie restoration area.

The emphasis in on the flora rather than the fauna at the Lincoln Memorial Garden, a living memorial to the nation's 16th president. Situated along the Lake Springfield shoreline, the garden offers five miles of trails through wooded groves, prairie grasses and wildflowers. Visitors can pause to contemplate nature—or one of the inspirational quotations from Abraham Lincoln carved into the garden's wooden benches. Designed in the 1930s by noted landscape architect Jens Jensen, the garden is maintained by a private foundation.

GOLF COURSES

When national interest in playing golf began burgeoning a few years ago, Springfield was at ground zero. Two brand-new courses, including a championship-grade course designed by tour pro Hale Irwin, opened in the past two years, and two more are in the planning stages. Meanwhile, existing courses continue to receive steady play.

Springfield is a haven for golfers, whether of the duffer or scratch variety. Virtually all residents live within a 10-minute drive of a public golf course. The park district and city operate two nine-hole courses and two 18-hole courses, all near comfortable, close-knit neighborhoods. The city courses are not only accessible—they're a bargain. City residents can play nine holes for less than $6. The recreation department's Lincoln Greens offers a more challenging experience, as well as glimpses of—and the occasional splash into—Lake Springfield.

Four privately operated, but publicly accessible, courses extend the opportunities even further. The newest, nine-hole Brookhills, is a tight, challenging course with bent-grass fairways and a

lighted driving range, conveniently located to accommodate the large population growth on Springfield's West Side. The 18-hole Rail, home of the Rail Charity Classic L.P.G.A. tournament, offers a long trek over well-manicured stretches, traps and bunkers amid one of Springfield's higher-end housing developments. The Oaks' 18 holes demand a full repertoire of golf shots, with holes that slope sharply between tight fairways as well as those that offer wide open spaces. Edgewood Golf Club in Auburn offers a unique and challenging 18-hole layout.

The city also has two private courses—the venerable Illini Country Club, course to Illinois governors, and Panther Creek, which opened in 1992 to a nearly full membership, many of whom live in the plush housing development at its perimeter.

PRO SPORTS

The biggest annual sporting event in Springfield is the Rail Charity Classic, one of the L.P.G.A.'s oldest continually operated tournaments. It is also one of the few that has survived without a major corporate backer, relying instead on support from a network of local business and community sponsors and a virtual army of volunteers.

The three-day tournament, held over the Labor Day weekend, generally draws national press coverage and a field of more than 120 women professional golfers, including some of the top names on the tour. The tourney has grown to encompass three companion events, including one of the L.P.G.A.'s most valuable "shootouts," and two pro-ams, one of which is for women only.

Baseball fans can visit Springfield's own field of dreams at Lanphier Park and watch the Class A Springfield Cardinals farm team play a 70-game home schedule from April through August. The 12 young men in the familiar redbird-on-the-bat uniforms represent the top 2 percent of young baseball talent in the Western Hemisphere. But the real game for most spectators lies in calculating which players will go up the road to the big leagues—or which will simply go home.

And though Springfield is about 90 miles from the nearest professional race track, the excitement of post time comes to town over closed-circuit television at the Capitol Teletrack Offtrack Betting Parlor. Patrons can place pari-mutuel wagers on major-stakes races from around the country, then

> **V**isitors can pause to contemplate nature—or one of the inspirational quotations from Abraham Lincoln.

Top: A bluegrass festival in New Salem, the rebuilt nineteenth-century town where Lincoln lived.

Bottom: A horn quartet takes advantage of the wonderful acoustics of the Old State Capitol.

watch the outcome on one of the 102 video monitors. The betting parlor also has facilities for dining and parties.

Amateur sports enthusiasts don't have to feel left out. In addition to publicly funded recreational programming and facilities, Springfield has an active YMCA, a YWCA, and dozens of private organizations and entrepreneurs in the business of providing fun. Highly popular softball and volleyball league play expanded recently to several area taverns after they made the happy discovery that ball diamonds and sand volleyball pits promote a healthy business environment. Private fitness clubs offer a multitude of ways to stay in shape. One of them even supplements the standard array of fitness equipment and routines with tennis and racquetball courts and an outdoor swimming pool.

The downtown YMCA maintains a large indoor swimming pool, men's and women's fitness centers, a day-care, and basketball, volleyball and racquetball courts. It also offers a wide variety of recreational programming, including swimming lessons for all ages and skill levels, gymnastics, basketball and volleyball leagues, a summer youth camp and a huge youth soccer program.

Family fun is also a specialty of Knight's Action Park, a private recreational development with a giant water slide, a go-cart track, two miniature golf courses, bumper boats and batting cages.

AREA ARTS AND CULTURE

The history of the arts in Springfield can be boiled down to a simple dynamic: someone saw a void—and filled it. The result has been the creation of an extremely active and diverse arts community. Springfield has an opera theater—and a group that performs spirituals. It has a symphony orchestra—and a group called Shining Riddims that brings internationally known reggae, Caribbean and African performers to town for charity benefits. It has a ballet—and an international folk-dancing group. Together, these groups offer the community a veritable smorgasbord of arts experiences that richly colors the fabric of life in Springfield.

In Springfield, the arts are as accessible as the parks. Restaurants, banks and many other public buildings double as galleries, and both the Illinois State Museum and the Springfield Art Association hold several exhibitions a year. Parks and other public places resound with music throughout the summer. And a variety of national historical and cultural treasures are almost always on view.

Citywide celebrations of the arts have given Springfield a unique set of traditions to mark the changing of the seasons. Tens of thousands of area residents salute the New Year at First Night Springfield, when government buildings, churches and businesses provide the settings for a downtown celebration of the arts. They flock downtown each May for the Old Capitol Art Fair, when the original town square becomes a huge outdoor art gallery. They celebrate Halloween with a costumed Springfield Symphony. And they close out the year with the Springfield Ballet's traditional performance of *The Nutcracker*.

And there is plenty to do in between. In the words of Rod Buffington, director of the Springfield Arts Association: "Springfield is very culturally rich. People can literally take in a different arts experience each night of the week and never repeat themselves all year long."

Many local arts groups and events derive major support from the Springfield Area Arts Council, which distributes grants from the Illinois Arts Council. It also promotes arts education through popular artist-in-residence programs, and the arts in general through various citywide efforts, including a banner program that beautifies the downtown while heralding upcoming arts events.

The council sponsors several arts occasions, including the Artist on the Plaza series of summer

In a switch on the usual practice, a participant in the annual Illinois State Fair has brought the bacon from home!

noontime concerts and two events that have become models for other cities, the annual Children's Art Fair and First Night Springfield.

Several other arts groups, however, have sprung into existence with little more than a dedicated audience for support. All in all, they give the region a rich potpourri of cultural offerings.

The Springfield Art Association, the city's most venerable arts group, was founded in 1913. It is headquartered in Edwards Place, a graceful Italianate mansion that was a center of mid-nineteenth century social life. Abraham Lincoln both politicked and socialized there. This rich historical site houses a collection of Victorian furniture and a permanent art collection. The art association also operates a school of art, with degreed instructors offering classes in a wide variety of media, including watercolor, oil and acrylic, pottery, textiles, jewelry and sculpture. The association sponsors a series of exhibitions each year, presents lectures and films and maintains one of the foremost art libraries in Illinois. Its art outreach program sends trained docents to bring

When it's time for the State Fair, Springfield becomes a country town again, rooted as it is in the richness and bounty of America's heartland.

portfolios of original art and reproductions to thousands of schoolchildren.

In recent years, the association also has sponsored the Fine Crafts Fair, which showcases the work of many nationally known crafts artists. And one of the highlights of Springfield's social scene is the annual Beaux Arts Ball, held for more than 50

years to honor key families who support the association with contributions and volunteer hours.

The cotillions and balls that were the height of fashion in nineteenth-century Springfield have given way to a milieu where just about any dance step is welcome.

The Springfield Ballet presents lavish productions of classical ballets, including popular favorites like *Cinderella* and *Sleeping Beauty*. It also showcases a sampling of modern dance, ballet, jazz and contemporary ballet. The company, one of the oldest in Illinois, develops and trains young dancers selected in annual tryouts, and brings the art of ballet to community organizations and area schools.

Whirling displays of color are a specialty of the Springfield International Folkdancers, who keep the diverse heritages of area residents alive and appreciated through dance. Members provide free lessons in Middle-European, English and American contra dances on Monday nights at the Lincoln Park Pavilion. Some members attend workshops to expand the group's repertoire, which has grown to include clogging and Turkish dancing.

The Prairie Grapevine's emphasis is on traditional American folk music and dance. Callers provide instruction at the group's regularly scheduled dances, which include hoedowns, New England contras, Appalachian big circles and couple dances. Local string bands provide live music.

Singers—and those who enjoy listening to them—can choose from a range of musical styles, including opera, of both the classical and the "muni" variety. The Opera Theater of Springfield, which offered its first production in 1981, has a repertoire ranging from *Die Fledermaus* to tragic *Carmen*. The group's ongoing educational program offers condensed versions of famous operas to area schoolchildren.

The city's *other* opera is the Springfield Muni Opera, which presents four rousing Broadway musicals each summer in an outdoor theater near Lake Springfield. While seating is available, many patrons choose to spread a blanket and watch the show from under the stars.

Vocal talent is also showcased in the Springfield Oratorio Choir, which was founded in 1971 to bring fine choral works to the Springfield area. The 40 to 60 members perform a traditional Christmas concert and a pops concert in June.

Another choir, Voices of Love, Joy and Peace,

emphasizes a highly American form of music, the spiritual. Based in Springfield's African-American community, the group is committed to preserving the singing and the story of this traditional form of sacred music. Members participate in programming for special events, including Dr. Martin Luther King's Birthday and Abraham Lincoln's Birthday.

One of the biggest recent expansions in the area arts menu has been within the theater community. The venerable Springfield Theater Center has provided quality theater and a creative outlet for live theater arts since 1947. It offers a wide range of productions and oversees both a formal training program and the White Rabbit Series, which is aimed at young audiences and features child performers in leading roles.

But several new groups have recently emerged to fill different audience niches. The happy result is that scarcely a weekend goes by when there isn't a play somewhere in town. One of the new groups is the Eastside Theater, formed mainly by members of Springfield's African-American community. Productions have created additional roles for black actors and have provided an eloquent forum for bringing attention to community concerns.

Fresh voices also are being heard from the Mid-America Playwrights Theater, which produces original plays, many written by local authors.

And central Illinois' historical legacy is center stage at the Great American People Show, which produces three original plays portraying the Lincoln legend. The group's repertoire began as outdoor performances in the summer only and has now expanded into a year-round schedule in a new indoor theater in New Salem State Park, just yards from the reconstructed village where Lincoln once lived.

The Springfield Symphony Orchestra, under the guidance of conductor Kenneth Keisler, is a professional ensemble of 85 musicians who perform more than 20 concerts each season. The symphony offers classical and pops concerts and free children's programs and family concerts, including a popular Halloween extravaganza that finds the whole orchestra in costume. The orchestra is complemented by the Springfield Symphony Chorus. Its crowning touch is the Illinois Chamber Orchestra, whose repertoire spans the literature of chamber music.

A junior version of the symphony is the Sangamon Valley Youth Symphony, a hand-picked group of 30 young people who perform for all age groups. Many members are well-known in area competitions, and several alumni have gone on to careers in music.

Springfield has been getting the blues as never before. Interest in blues has grown tremendously in the last few years, due partly to the efforts of the

Illinois Central Blues Club. The club provides local blues musicians a chance to jam on "Blue Monday" at local clubs. Its annual festival features nationally and internationally known blues musicians.

Some of the most regular settings for live music are local restaurants and nightclubs, which feature programs of everything from rock to jazz to country to polka tunes. One of the biggest musical programs of the year is the eclectic lineup at the Illinois State Fair. And the Sangamon State University Auditorium hosts about 60 performances a year, including a broad spectrum of music, dance and theater. The Prairie Capital Convention Center offers another large venue for nationally known acts.

As a city with a rich past, Springfield has a wealth of buildings with both historical and architectural meaning. Pre-eminent among them is the comparatively modest Lincoln Home, which draws visitors from around the world.

However, the city also is home to an important house designed by the great architect Frank Llyod Wright. Built in 1903 by a flamboyant heiress, Susan Lawrence Dana, the house, now known as the Dana-Thomas House, contains hundreds of priceless artifacts, including many of the original furnishings designed by Wright himself. A

The place is the First Drummer, and the sound is *jazz*.

painstaking renovation, completed by the state in 1991 at a cost of $5 million, has restored the house to its heyday as a Springfield social center and showplace.

Illinois' capital since 1837, Springfield also is the site of the state's fourth and fifth statehouse

Above: Over and out!

Opposite: Fireworks bursting in air over the illuminated dome of the Illinois State Capitol.

the first designed specifically to house the state's collection of library materials.

Still more clues to the past can be found in the nearby Archives Building, built in 1938 to protect the state's valuable historic records from theft, fire and the weather. A climate-controlled vault contains all of the papers connected with Lincoln's legislative career, including documents in his own writing.

A few steps away is the Illinois State Museum, which showcases the state's natural and cultural history. Visitors are welcomed by a replica of a Tlingit Indian totem pole, topped by a carving of a powerful chieftan, Abraham Lincoln. The museum curates several art exhibitions a year and offers several programs for young patrons.

History comes to life at three other sites that evoke life in the mid-nineteenth century. The Clayville Rural Life Center features a restored 1850s stagecoach stop. Festivals staged there by the Clayville Folk Arts Guild offer a colorful glimpse of prairie life and pioneer arts and crafts.

buildings. The building currently in use is a silver-domed Italianate structure, which celebrated its 100th birthday in 1988. The richly detailed building displays murals and statues galore that depict important moments in Illinois history.

The Old State Capitol exhibits the more restrained Greek Revival style of architecture. Site of Lincoln's immortal "house divided against itself" speech, the building was meticulously restored to its original appearance, inside and out, after serving for years as the county courthouse. Candlelight tours by docents dressed in period costume are a special treat.

Springfield is a treasure trove for anyone with an interest in the past. The city is home to the stately Illinois State Library, which contains a wealth of reference materials and the genealogical key to the past of many Illinois families. Completed in 1990 at a cost of $37 million, the building is

Civil war buffs can contemplate the past at the Grand Army of the Republic Memorial Museum and the Daughters of the Union Veterans of the Civil War Museum. While miles from a battlefield, Springfield has a grim reminder of the consequences of the nation's greatest conflict. Camp Butler Cemetery, once the site of a Union training camp and Confederate prison, is now a cemetery for veterans and their dependents.

The days when Lincoln studied law and was elected as a state legislator are evoked at Lincoln's New Salem, a reconstructed village of log cabins. Riverboat rides on a flatboat similar to the one that brought Lincoln to town, are offered on the nearby Sangamon River—"if the creek don't rise."

7

Partners in Excellence

SPRINGFIELD HAS ALWAYS been a model of economic diversity—from its early days as a frontier outpost to its present role as a thriving metropolitan area and the capital of Illinois. Characterized by ingenuity, perseverance, and concern for the future, today's businesses and organizations provide goods and services to the local, national, and international marketplace.

The following pages present the enterprises whose participation made this book possible. Arranged categorically, these businesses and organizations reflect the wide range of opportunities that Springfield has to offer. The first category is Networks, beginning on page 78. The other sections include Business and Professions, 85; Manufacturing, 104; Real Estate and Development, 109; Marketplace, 116; and Quality of Life, 130.

Each of these participants offers unique contributions that enrich the environment enjoyed by Springfield residents and visitors alike.

Letting the light in at Sangamon State University's Public Affairs Center.

Chicago & Illinois Midland Railroad

The Chicago and Illinois Midland Railway (C&IM), a 121-mile rail carrier running from Peoria to Taylorville, is the only railroad with its general offices located in Springfield. The C&IM offers shippers an exceptional array of logistical options, beginning with neutral connections to 11 transcontinental, regional, and switching railroads.

The C&IM's heritage dates back to September 1888 when the Pawnee Railroad was chartered. This original road was four miles long, running from Pawnee to the Pawnee Junction (now called Cimic), where the road connected with the St. Louis & Chicago Railroad. An additional five miles were added by May 1892, allowing the first train to run from Pawnee to Auburn on June 1, 1892.

In 1905 The Illinois Midland Coal Company, associated with the Chicago Edison Company (now Commonwealth Edison) and the Peabody Coal Company, purchased the Pawnee Railroad to transport coal from central Illinois to the Chicago area. Illinois Midland Coal Company changed the railroad's name to the Central Illinois Railway Company; however, to avoid confusion with the nearby Illinois Central Railroad, the name was changed to the Chicago & Illinois Midland Railway Company, taking the name of its corporate parents: Chicago Edison Company and Illinois Midland Coal Company.

By 1917 the C&IM connected with the Chicago and the North Western Railway, allowing direct access to Commonwealth Edison's plants in the Chicago area and giving the C&IM its fourth direct connection with Chicago.

As a principal coal hauler for Commonwealth Edison, the C&IM receives coal from connecting carriers at Peoria and delivers it to Powerton or to Havana, where it is then transloaded into barges destined for Chicago-area generating stations.

Today the C&IM transports nearly four million tons of coal annually, which accounts for approximately 85 percent of the railroad's traffic. Other shipments include grain, food products, feed, lumber, fertilizer, and scrap iron. Other major customers include American Milling, Cargill, Solomon Chem-Grind, and Reed Mineral. Total carloadings are approximately 48,000 per year, and the C&IM offers regular freight service between Peoria and Taylorville, via Springfield. Additional coal trains are operated as necessary to Powerton and Havana to meet the needs of its customers.

The C&IM currently owns 19 locomotives and 133 freight cars, with ready access to a full range of freight equipment. In addition, it has full EDI capabilities for billing and car location. The railroad is also operating a major, new rail/truck lumber transfer in Springfield to serve lumber customers in central Illinois and Indiana.

With accessible railway lines and extensive transfer and transload capabilities, the C&IM is uniquely positioned to continue its reliable and cost-effective transportation of staples and commodities throughout the continental United States. With more than a century of experience, well-maintained track and equipment, experienced personnel, and competitive rates, the C&IM continues its commitment to ensure stable transportation service to connect its Midwest industries to their national and international suppliers and customers.

....

Above:

C&IM Work Extra Number 18 South on its way to Reed Mineral and the Christian County landfill just after crossing the Lake Springfield Bridge located on the ICRR.

Right:

C&IM Work Extra Number 71 North leaves Springfield with cars to be delivered to PPU RR at Peoria daily. In the foreground is the C&IM tower and depot at 15th and North Grand.

....

Springfield Mass Transit District

As a city grows, so grows its transportation system, and the growth of the city of Springfield parallels the growth of the Springfield Mass Transit District. The Springfield area, consisting of Capitol, Springfield, and Woodside townships, comprises the Springfield Mass Transit District (SMTD), which was created in July 1968 by a referendum vote in accordance with the Local Mass Transit Act of the State of Illinois.

Since its inception the SMTD has successfully pursued its mission: to transport the citizens of Springfield. From schoolchildren to the elderly, people have traveled from almost any point in the Springfield area to another, for 50 cents or less.

The origin of public bus service for the city began in 1923 with the preparation of Springfield's first city plan, which specified the need for mass transit, or in those days, streetcar lines. For many years streetcars and trolleys took Springfield workers to and from work. In December 1937, however, the last streetcar carried passengers across town, and the city buses took over.

Today the SMTD consists of a fleet of 46 buses. The service employs more than 90 people. Every Monday through Saturday, 12 main routes are driven 6:00 a.m. to 6:00 p.m., with the exception of holidays. These routes are the same as the original trolley routes, operating in a "hub-and-spoke" configuration to and from downtown Springfield. Additional routes have been added as needed, such as to the Greyhound bus terminal and other high-demand areas. The SMTD also runs a shuttle service for Illinois State Fair and Air Rendezvous goers.

As the city has developed with White Oaks, White Oaks Plaza, Parkway Pointe, and other suburbs, as well as the addition of the Bloom Office Building and the Teachers Retirement Complex, the SMTD has re-evaluated its current system. Affected by the movement of the population, the SMTD will begin a major impact study to determine what the Springfield area needs in the way of convenience, speed, and accessibility in a public transportation line.

Ridership is varied and the SMTD caters to all. As the population grows older the demand for bus service for the elderly has increased. The SMTD buses are equipped with wheelchair lifts for disabled people and senior citizens.

Door-to-door service is also possible with the Access Illinois Transit System. The AITS buses are smaller, van-type vehicles with personalized schedules for otherwise homebound citizens.

Disabled people and seniors ride for half the usual fare. With schools and day-care centers spread all over the area, more children also are riding the buses. Children younger than four years old ride for free.

The SMTD also reflects the city's environmental needs. Operation Clean Ride is a pollution-reducing program the SMTD and the Central Illinois Light Company are pursuing. This project involves AITS and CILCO vehicles converted from gas to compressed natural gas operation.

As the city and its transportation needs change, the SMTD continues to provide the best possible services to the citizens of Springfield.

Above:
SMTD operates one of the newer bus fleets in Illinois. The useful life of buses, such as the one pictured here, is 12 years. The average age of the SMTD fleet is 6 years.

Left:
Preventive maintenance is a primary concern at SMTD. The buses represent a $6.5 million investment, and much time and effort are spent to ensure that the vehicles last as long as possible.

WMAY-WNNS

"**W**hat we do best is serve the community," says Thomas Kushak, president and general manager of radio stations WMAY and WNNS. That service may include local or national news, weather reports, public service announcements, raising money for needy organizations, or even musical entertainment. The definition of service changes every day, driven by community needs.

Kushak also points to his station's 16-year history of airing local editorials as a community contribution. "Our goal is to cause people to think and to act, not to win them over to our way of thinking," he remarks.

WMAY, at 970 AM, went on the air October 15, 1950, after a dedication highlighted by the appearance of Governor Adlai Stevenson. An affiliate of the National Broadcasting Corporation (NBC) since 1952, the station is also affiliated with Cable News Network (CNN) and Dow Jones Network.

WMAY promises "Weather reports every 15 minutes" and continuous news coverage when local or national events dictate. Kushak emphasizes news and information as WMAY's major commitment, only switching to 1950s and 1960s music— "Great Oldies"—after all current news is fully covered.

WNNS, known as "Lite Rock 99," can be found at 98.7 FM. With its adult contemporary format, WNNS broadcasts within a 60-mile radius of Springfield. Airing first in 1980 as a stand-alone station, WNNS was purchased by WMAY three years later. Kushak points out that the "Lite Rock/ Less Talk" format consistently garners more adult listeners than any other Springfield-area station.

Both stations are highly visible across central Illinois as a result of service projects and listener promotions.

Throughout the year, WMAY and WNNS can be found collecting donations of food for local food pantries, leading fund drives for special pro-

motions, organizing major community events, and involving station personnel in a multitude of local boards and service clubs.

While deeply committed to all community service projects, Kushak expressed his greatest pride in having raised more than $500,000 for the American Cancer Society through WMAY-WNNS' Jail 'N Bail, and more than $200,000 for local charities with the WNNS/VALCO Cruise for Charity.

In addition to WMAY-WNNS' continued emphasis on community service, both stations continue to make major technical improvements. Using all available digital technology, "Our goal is to broadcast a signal as close to compact-disc quality as possible," says Kushak. WMAY takes pride in being the first Springfield-area station to broadcast in AM stereo.

WMAY and WNNS are affiliated with "Mid-West Family"—an 18-station broadcasting company operated locally as Long Nine, Inc. Kushak explains the "Family" in the group's parent name is indicative of its pride in local station's ownership and the local family of employees. "Radio is a people business," Kushak says, "and if you have the great people, you have great radio stations— stations that take their public trust very seriously and make a major commitment to the community." Kushak expresses special pride in the 45 full- and part-time employees who give WMAY and WNNS their "competitive edge" in a highly competitive industry.

City of Springfield

Springfield is a nurturing place—a city in which dreams, children, livelihoods, and gardens grow equally well.

Springfield feels like a small town, but it also happens to be a capital city. It is a city where you can leave home early on a summer morning; pick a pint of fresh wild raspberries; return home for a shower, a change of clothes, a breakfast of the raspberries—and still make it to work on time.

Springfield can be a seat of controversy. It was both home to the Great Emancipator and the site of race riots and bigotry, which roared through its heart decades ago. It became a city that dissolved one system of government and replaced it with a system that more fairly accommodates those residents who were once persecuted.

Springfield's largest parks are magnificent tributes to their founders—true parks, rather than walled compounds surrounded by urban chaos. Smaller parks, which dot the city, are the focus of rest and recreation for nearby residents of all ages.

Springfield was built upon a legacy. Founded in the middle of a prairie, it offered warmth, security, and comfort to its new residents. Even before Abraham Lincoln called the city his home, it featured a logical grid of streets that remains today.

In many ways, Springfield mirrored the growth of the country— as the railroads, the mines, and the industries grew, then waned, then came to terms with the needs of a modern people.

Today Springfield offers what many homeowners look for in their city. Public and private educational opportunities exist for students of every age. A common infrastructure works well to connect people and bring them services they cannot create for themselves. Electricity and water are provided inexpensively by the largest and oldest municipally-owned utility in Illinois.

Springfield offers its residents a rainbow of entertainment choices; rock concerts and symphony concerts; national touring companies and local ballet productions; and annual street festivals, summer or winter.

The area's labor force is a stable 109,000 workers, who are available year-round and have a broad base of skills. Even during the recent economic recession, unemployment hovered around an enviable five percent. Hundreds of construction projects are undertaken every year; and in a recent year, when national housing sales plummeted, the local numbers rose to more than 2,425 houses sold. Total retail sales climbed steadily throughout the past decade to more than $1.5 billion.

Springfield is a nurturing place—where peoples of the past have created a legacy that has become the city of today—where the people of today prepare a legacy for the city of tomorrow.

Springfield is built upon a legacy. Today, in many ways, this capital city feels like a small town. It offers many move-weary homeowners a chance to nurture their own roots and contribute to the city of tomorrow.

Central Illinois Light Company

The Springfield Division Customer Advisory Council of this Peoria-based firm was created in 1985. Made up of customers from CILCO's southern service territory, the Council discusses issues affecting customer service, tours facilities and talks with company managers. Activities include recommending more effective customer communications and suggesting ways to explain the complex utility business.

In 1987, CILCO "adopted" Matheny School in Springfield. As CILCO employees tutored students, they became aware of the challenges of working with students from various cultural backgrounds. CILCO turned these challenges into the opportunity to develop a Multi-Cultural Center for use by all district teachers. Opened at Matheny in 1989, the Center houses materials which address teaching students from diverse cultural heritages.

Operation Clean Ride is a joint effort by CILCO, the Springfield Mass Transit District (SMTD) and the Sangamon Valley Chapter of the American Red Cross. It began in 1990 as a direct response to concerns about the environment and dependence on foreign oil. Selected Red Cross vehicles used to transport the handicapped and some equipment used by SMTD were converted to run on compressed natural gas. Using this safe, economical and virtually pollution-free transportation fuel reduces dependence on foreign oil. CILCO will monitor the pilot project, which is expected to improve mileage and reduce maintenance.

CILCO has also received recognition for local participation in the arts. In 1989, the company received the Mayor's Award for the Arts in the corporate division. This award praised the company's support of established art groups and its efforts to seek out new activities. A year later, CILCO received the Sydney R. Yates Arts Advocacy Award from the Illinois Arts Alliance Foundation and the Outstanding Corporation Award from the Central Illinois Chapter of the National Society of Fund Raising Executives.

These people-centered activities are worlds away from the gas production goals of CILCO's ancestor companies. The Peoria Gas Light and Coke Company was granted an organization charter in 1853. The Springfield Gas Light Company was organized in 1854 and became one of more than a dozen utilities which now make up Central Illinois Light Company.

Those were the days in which coal usage was measured in bushels instead of tons, when streets were lighted by gas fixtures and the annual value of products manufactured was less than $20,000. It was an era before electric power generation and studies of solar energy, when environmental concerns were minimal and energy audits were unknown. Yet as CILCO grew, the company blended these and other technological advances with community-wide interests and concerns. Proud of these advancements, CILCO looks forward to bringing warmth and light in many ways throughout the communities it serves.

Above:
CILCO, in a pilot project with the Springfield Mass Transit District and the Sangamon Valley chapter of the the American Red Cross, has converted several A.I.T.S. vehicles to run on compressed natural gas, a safe, economical, and virtually pollution-free fuel.
Right:
CILCO's community srevice projects include employee volunteer tutoring for students of Matheny Elementary School, the company's "adopted" school. CILCO has promoted the Adopt-A-School Program in Springfield's annual Christmas parade.

WICS TV-20

News coverage is a primary ingredient in the program mix of WICS TV-20. In the past decade the station has doubled the news aired each week and doubled its news budget to reflect this emphasis.

The station provides early risers with a half-hour local newscast at 6:30 a.m. and can now broadcast simultaneously from five locations. In addition TV-20 is one of fewer than three dozen stations nationwide to provide real-time closed captioning of local newscasts.

The 20 News staff works to explain and clarify the significance of news events to viewers within its 16-county viewing area. This may take the form of interviews with the people actually affected by major news events, or it could involve an extended series of news features.

TV-20's debut programming was the "World Series Baseball Classic" on September 30, 1953. It was an era when, other than shows from the NBC network, all programming was broadcast live—including commercials. In 1962 videotape technology enabled TV-20 to record commercials and local programs for later broadcast. The station

began receiving network television signals through a satellite distribution system in 1985.

Guy Gannett Publishing Company of Portland, Maine, owns WICS-TV, three other television stations, and 29 newspapers. Each of these operations independently decides the extent of its community involvement.

Beyond its broadcast functions, WICS TV-20 serves as a strong thread in the fabric of life for more than one million people in the station's Total Survey Area. In partnership with other leading local institutions, TV-20 community initiatives concentrate on education, health, environment, and the arts. More than a dozen community projects include:

• Books for Beginners: collection and distribution of used children's books;
• Coats for Kids: collection and distribution of used children's coats;
• Black History Month: vignettes highlighting the contributions of black Americans;
• Partners in Health: half-hour special reports on local health care issues;
• Earthwatch: environmental messages focused on recycling;
• Santa's Friends: collection of thousands of stuffed animals for needy children at Christmas;
• Sponsorship of Springfield Ballet Company performances and shows at Muni Opera, Sangamon State University, and Springfield Theater Center.

In its four decades of broadcasting, WICS TV-20 has grappled with changing technology and changing viewer concerns. The station fully intends to continue bringing local issues to area viewers and to address a wide spectrum of needs in the Springfield area and throughout Lincolnland.

....
Above:
During four decades of broadcasting, WICS TV-20 has teamed up with other local institutions to promote initiatives in education, health, environment, and the arts.
Left:
The evening news anchors at WICS TV-20 are (sitting from left) Don Hickman, Susan Finzen, (standing from left) Gus Gordon, and Paul Wappel. A primary news goal is to explain the local significance of major news events to viewers in the station's 16-county viewing area.
....

Illinois Times

"**W**e try to offer information readers can't find anyplace else, topics that aren't covered elsewhere, and writing of the type that isn't offered in other media," explains *Illinois Times* publisher Fletcher Farrar, Jr. *Illinois Times* is also a lower-cost alternative for advertisers who target the paper's 30,000 educated and active readers.

Illinois Times first went to press in 1975, and Farrar bought it two years later. Although the question arose frequently during the weekly's youth, after 17 years nobody asks if the paper will survive. One measure of the paper's success is the fact that readers grab it up so quickly.

There are more than 200 distribution points in and around Springfield, so readers make a conscious decision to pick up each free issue. Many distribution points are stripped of their current edition just a day after each Thursday's delivery.

The *Illinois Times*' South Seventh Street office is an old Victorian house, purchased in 1978 from the Women's Christian Temperance Union. With its restored entrance, hardwood floors, and turn-of-the-century light fixtures, the office exemplifies one of the publication's frequent editorial topics—historical preservation through adaptive building reuse.

As an alternative newsweekly, *Illinois Times* holds its own because "we do things differently, not just the same things faster," Farrar explains. Usually avoiding such mass gatherings as news conferences, IT's writers "don't cover everything, but we try to cover our topics in depth." Despite the thinking of some readers, *Illinois Times* does not go out of its way to create debate, Farrar emphasizes. "We just try to tell the truth—which sometimes results in controversy." In the same breath he admits, "We don't shy away from controversy." *Illinois Times* writers offer opinions which are largely missing from the rest of the local market. Whether readers agree is immaterial, since the more information and opinions they see, the better they will be able to draw their own conclusions, Farrar explains.

Perhaps because of Springfield's highly political atmosphere, with roots that trace back to Abraham Lincoln, this market is a good area in which to foster differing ideas. *Illinois Times* enjoys building on this tradition of tolerance, and hopes that the paper's occasional dissent from the mainstream serves as a catalyst for involvement.

As a founding member of the nationwide Association of Alternative Newsweeklies, Farrar sees examples of alternative weekly journalism in many markets where competing dailies previously existed. He notes that few towns the size of Springfield actively support an alternative weekly in the same market as a daily paper. He joins with the staff in relishing the challenges that come from scrutinizing local news to find what's been left out—and then supplying the missing pieces.

Bank One, Springfield

"Whatever it takes" is the philosophy of Illinois' oldest bank, Bank One, Springfield. Whatever it takes, that is, to continue a tradition of meeting and exceeding customers' expectations. Even Abraham Lincoln ranks among its many satisfied customers, maintaining an account at the bank from 1853 until his assassination.

Since opening its doors in 1851 as the Springfield Marine and Fire Insurance Company, Bank One, Springfield has fostered a sound reputation for service, quality, and stability. Even during the Great Depression, Bank One, then known as the Springfield Marine Bank, continued its tradition of service to customers and stockholders.

Over the decades, the bank expanded its services, establishing the Trust Department in 1920, Farm and Consumer Loan Departments in the early 1930s, and the Investment Department in the early 1940s. By 1981, after 130 years of service, the bank's assets topped $500 million, making it the first bank in Illinois, outside of Chicago, to reach this level.

In 1992, along with affiliate offices in Bloomington-Normal, Champaign-Urbana, Monticello, DeLand, and Taylorville, the bank merged with BANC ONE CORPORATION. Sharing similar cultures, markets, and goals, the union of these two strong banking organizations enhances and ensures quality customer service for Central Illinois residents.

BANC ONE holds an outstanding record of 20 years of increased earnings, a record unsurpassed among the nation's 50 largest banking organizations. A pioneer in introducing new products and services, BANC ONE is structured as a multibank holding company, with each affiliate having its own chief executive and board of directors. The integration of local autonomy and multibank innovation offers customers of Bank One, Springfield, a broader array of services, a larger number of regional locations, and ongoing access to the latest technology.

A combination of conservative lending, innovative technology, and remarkable customer service is the hallmark of Bank One, Springfield. Local savings, checking, and credit services are the mainstays of Bank One, providing a strong foundation for continued growth. With government, higher education, health care, and insurance as the economic backbones of the communities it serves, Bank One excels in delivering traditional personal and corporate products, as well as innovative non-credit services including trust, farm management, and corporate cash management.

A high level of community involvement is also a top priority for Bank One. A citywide Student of the Year program and the Willard Bunn, Jr., and Urban League scholarships represent the bank's corporate commitment to education. Active participation of employees in numerous local organizations exhibits Bank One's dedication to community development. Bank One's sponsorship of cultural exhibitions, plays, and touring groups enriches the quality of life in central Illinois.

A thorough knowledge of its customers, an established presence in central Illinois, electronic capability serving major companies nationwide, and a solid capital position ensure that Bank One, Springfield will continue to provide its customers with "whatever it takes" to meet the challenges of the future.

A Springfield tradition for more than 140 years, Bank One, Springfield's home office is located on the east side of Old State Capitol Plaza.

The Greater Springfield Chamber of Commerce

Today's Greater Springfield Chamber of Commerce is a descendant of the Springfield Board of Trade, established in 1869. The lineage is by no means direct, however; over the years many business organizations diverged and reconverged to form the foundation of today's 1,500-member Chamber.

Formed more than 100 years ago by local business individuals who foresaw the advantage of joining together for business enhancement and prosperity, the present Chamber is governed by 24 volunteers on the board of directors, most elected from chamber membership to three-year terms. Three directors are appointed by board consent annually. This board administers policy and makes all decisions in the interest of the members.

The board's charge is to implement the annual Program of Work, a comprehensive action plan for the Greater Springfield community, through the efforts of volunteers on a variety of standing committees and affiliate boards. Standing committees include those of the ambassadors, education, finance, government action, manufacturers, nominations, public relations, small business, trans-

portation, and utilities and environment. In addition, ad hoc committees include community infrastructure, work force preparation, agribusiness, Plae Dae, and the John George Nicolay Secretary's Seminar. Affiliate organizations are the Governor's Prayer Breakfast, Economic Development Council (EDC), Springfield Central Area Development Association (SCADA), the Leadership Springfield Institute, and Springfield Downtown Parking, Inc.

In some ways today's chamber is very much like its predecessors. Business retention and economic development are as important to the chamber today as they were to the Springfield Citizens Improvement Association in 1889. The Improvement Association encouraged and promoted the growth and improvement of the City of Springfield and Sangamon County. The mission of today's chamber is to enhance the business climate and to promote and stimulate orderly economic growth within Sangamon County.

One important function of this economic focus is to attract new businesses to the area. Brochures, economic surveys, fact sheets, and reports, prepared in 1912 by the Springfield Commercial Association, served to acquaint the outside world with the city of Springfield, its advantages, resources, and opportunities. Today's sophisticated print materials are supplemented by videos and slide presentations, but the chamber's overall purpose is largely unchanged.

Another important function of the chamber is the retention and expansion of existing businesses. More than 125 businesses are visited annually to gather information and identify the needs of Springfield's business community. Demographic information, business attitude surveys, and other support services are provided. The chamber continuously checks the economic pulse of Sangamon County to retain its vitality and viability.

Involvement in government affairs is a third major chamber function. The annual Washing-

Below:

The monthly *UPDATE* magazine provides the chamber's 1,500-plus members with key information on legislation, organizational activities, and economic developments in the community.

ton Fly-In provides an opportunity to meet with lawmakers and other officials. The chamber has taken stands on issues such as the Clean Air Act, sewer rehabilitation, solid waste management, school district capital improvements, Hunter Lake, and State Road Fund diversions.

These examples parallel involvement by predecessors in establishment of the Springfield Sanitary District, campaigning for local political reform, representation at freight rate hearings, purchase of Lincoln's home for donation to the state, construction of Lake Springfield, and acquiring state assistance to build the Convention Center.

A fourth major chamber function is to serve as a community information and referral source. Almost 3,000 requests arrive annually by phone and mail from schoolchildren, tourists, and businesses. Questions such as "Who is the mayor of Illinois?" "Where is a good ethnic restaurant?" and "How many housing starts were there in Sangamon County last year?" are each given a thoughtful reply.

A fifth function of the Greater Springfield Chamber of Commerce is to provide a common and collective voice for the business community. As such, the chamber is a reflection of the nation's business climate and trends. Today's membership, for example, reflects global trends toward diversified small businesses rather than domination by large industries or financial institutions. The large majority of chamber members represent small businesses. Younger people join the chamber readily and about half of its members are women. Environmental and social issues are surfacing as business, not just community, issues.

Completing many of the tasks generated by these chamber functions is the job of its small but

dedicated staff of 17 employees. Three departments conduct the daily operations of the chamber: economic development, member services, and operations.

The chamber also produces a monthly newsletter, *UPDATE*, which keeps the membership informed of activities and current business issues. Special mailings also announce chamber events, meetings, and business-related legislation. All members are listed in the annual publication "Membership Directory & Executive Calendar," which is distributed to more than 3,500 area businesses, individuals, and community newcomers.

In the front of the line of The Greater Springfield Chamber is a core of hardworking, dependable volunteers. Hundreds of members make up the volunteer foundation of the chamber and serve on standing and affiliated committees, as well as work on special projects and events that arise throughout the year.

The chamber is formally accredited by the U.S. Chamber of Commerce, and its work is recognized as exemplary. Of the 5,000 Chambers of Commerce nationwide, the local chamber is one of only about eight percent to be nationally accredited. The chamber first received accreditation in 1982. Since then, every five years dozens of members volunteer hundreds of hours in a rigorous process of assessing the organization's capabilities and commitment in meeting established standards of organizational integrity, business programs, and professional capabilities.

A tradition of pulling together to affect positive change for the welfare of the community, its people, and its business provides the focal point for the chamber's direction and directives. The chamber is responsible for enhancing unity and pride and creating and retaining business development and jobs.

The Greater Springfield Chamber of Commerce will continue to improve the quality of life and work in Sangamon County.

Left:
The chamber's office is strategically located at Three South Old State Capitol Plaza at the center of Springfield's downtown business district.
Below Left:
The Greater Springfield Chamber, the state's third-largest business organization, is the recognized voice of the area's employment community.

Magna Bank of Central Illinois

Magna Bank of Central Illinois, N.A., is a $650-million commercial bank with primary locations in Springfield, Decatur, Bloomington, and Lincoln, Illinois.

The bank is part of Magna Group, Inc., a four-billion-dollar multibank holding company serving Illinois and Missouri from 98 retail banking locations. The resources of the holding company, coupled with the talents and professional expertise of skilled local bankers, offer Magna customers the finest in personal and commercial banking service. The Springfield banking center operates from three convenient locations: the main bank at 1825 South Sixth Street and facilities at Fourth and South Grand Avenue and 111 S. Durkin Drive.

Thomas B. Curtright, executive vice president and branch manager of the Springfield operation, describes Magna's pioneering spirit. "In our earlier years, we were the first bank to offer suburban drive-up banking, the first to offer full-service Saturday hours, and the first to offer our own bank credit card. More recently, the bank has been a leader in electronic automated-teller service and in the development of imaginative new services designed for specific customer groups." Club Magna 55, for people 55 years or older, expands the typical role of the bank from just a provider of financial services to a social organization. There are more than 4,000 members in Club Magna 55 enjoying this special package of banking services, informative seminars, tours, and trips.

The Magna Advantage Account also has more than 4,000 members. This special group of customers enjoys the benefits of unlimited checking privileges, free personalized advantage checks, an automatic-teller machine card with no annual fee, a MasterCard and VISA card with no annual fee, along with many other free or discounted banking services, including special insurance coverage.

Magna is proud of its continuing strong presence in Springfield and central Illinois. Curtright emphasizes, "Our bank demonstrates a care and concern, not only for the large commercial customer borrowing millions for a new plant, but also for the small business person or homeowner needing a new roof." Magna's loans finance homes, automobiles, home improvements, and the needs of commerce—all within the local market. The strategy is simple: The deposits gathered from the local market are used for the benefit of Springfield. Curtright explains, "We've never lost our link with the Springfield community. Our success is based on Springfield's success."

Above:
Magna Bank of Central Illinois continues to introduce new, imaginative retail services designed for specific customer groups.
Right:
Financing for Illinois Plumbing and Heating Supply Company's new, 30,000-square-foot warehouse and showroom was provided by Magna Bank of Central Illinois.

Standard Mutual Insurance Company

Standard Mutual Insurance Company was founded by Frank Roberts in 1921 to write automobile insurance exclusively. With only a small number of registered automobiles and less than 3,000 miles of paved highways in Illinois, Standard Mutual became one of the early pioneers in automobile insurance. Frank Roberts was the guiding force in the company's early development. His son, Mark O. Roberts, Sr., joined the company as general counsel in 1934, and later was named president in 1953. Together they established a prestigious record of growth based on quality insurance and personal service.

Standard Mutual's steady growth over the years required three moves, the last one in 1956 to its current location on the corner of MacArthur Boulevard and South Grand Avenue West. In that same year, the firm expanded into Indiana, as well as into multiple lines of insurance.

Mark O. Roberts, Sr., current chairman of the board, has been active in both insurance and law, serving as a member of the Illinois State Board of Law Examiners; Special Assistant Attorney General, State of Illinois (1953-1961); past president of the Sangamon County Bar Association; and a member of various legal associations. In recognition of his and Standard Mutual's many contributions to the community, a new addition to the home office, which approximately doubled the

size of usable office space, was dedicated to him on May 15, 1981. It was officially declared "Mark O. Roberts Day" by the City of Springfield.

Mark O. Roberts, Jr., CPCU, MBA, joined the firm in 1969, becoming the third generation of Roberts family management. He became executive vice president of Standard Mutual in 1981 and was named president on June 1, 1992, as his father's successor. Mark Jr. is also very active in the Springfield community, serving on the board of directors of Town & Country Bank, in addition to being a corporation member of Memorial Medical Center, a trustee of the Springfield Public Schools Foundation, and a member of various insurance associations.

Standard Mutual employees participate in many community events, such as the March of Dimes Team Walk America event. In 1992, for the fifth consecutive year, Standard Mutual won the March of Dimes' traveling trophy for the most contributions collected. The employees take justifiable pride in this accomplishment.

Selling policies exclusively through professional independent agents, Standard Mutual has a proven record as a multiple-line company offering the best service in all property and casualty lines. It has consistently received an "A" (Excellent) rating from A.M. Best Company and has regional offices in Indianapolis, Indiana, and Oak Brook, Illinois.

Plans for the future include the addition of other insurance lines, continued development of innovative services and products, and further expansion in the Midwest. Standard Mutual continues its original business principle of "quality insurance and personal service at reasonable rates," as it has for more than 71 years, which ensures its leadership in the insurance industry.

Above:
Mark O. Roberts, Sr., the portrait of Frank Roberts, and Mark O. Roberts, Jr., represent three generations of Roberts family management. Other members of the management team are William Ascroft, Jr., secretary-treasurer and chief financial officer; James A. Schultz, vice president-underwriting; James W. Theis, vice president-finance; Wiliam M. Gibbons, claims manager; and Robert Warner, data-processing manager. Mark Sr. and Mark Jr. also serve on the board of directors with attorney Hugh J. Graham, banker Noah T. Herndon, William Ascroft, Jr., and Kathryn F. Martin.

Below left:
In 1956 construction began at the southwest corner of MacArthur Boulevard and South Grand Avenue West for the present home office facility, a handsome building with a soft, red-brick exterior in the Williamsburg style. A major addition completed in 1981 on the company's 60th anniversary, matches the main building in architectural style.

United Trust, Inc.

United Trust, Inc., is a product of sound investments, insurance protection, and growth. United Trust, Inc., is a Springfield-based insurance holding company with one principal operating subsidiary, United Trust Group, and two additional affiliates. It is a firm that owes its success largely to the fact

that Illinois people have invested in Illinois.

Since its organization in 1984 its staff has developed a distinctive marketing approach and deliberate planning strategies to create a dramatic success story. United Trust, Inc., has focused on four strategic goals:
• Stable investment growth for shareholders;
• Secure, successful careers for each member of a growing work force;
• Protection for policyholders;
• Resources to conduct company affairs as a conscientious corporate citizen.

Its initial pattern of growth has become familiar now, repeating itself with only minor variations on the original theme. Recent acquisitions of other insurance firms and insurance holding companies have resulted in the creation of an insurance group with $370 million in assets.

This has become feasible because from the outset United Trust reinforced its planning with a

secure economic base. The first corporate goal of the firm's organizers, Larry E. Ryherd and Thomas F. Morrow, was secure funding. In just two years the corporation raised $15 million through an Illinois intrastate offering. This total was more than double the six-million-dollar capitalization record reached previously in the State of Illinois, and significantly more than the known previous national capitalization record of $10 million.

The strategy for that stock offering continues to be reflected in the company's expansion. Through a survey, management identified professional, business, and farming leaders in all 102 Illinois counties. Almost 6,500 people eagerly took advantage of the opportunity to invest in this new company.

Once the stock offering was completed in 1987, the initial sales force was relicensed to offer insurance products through the life insurance firm, United Trust Assurance Company (UTAC).

The initial United Trust, Inc., stockholders served both as a core for offering insurance and as a referral network through which the sales force continued to contact leaders within each county.

The company has grown well beyond the boundaries of Illinois, however. UTAC also offers insurance products in Indiana, Kentucky, Mis-

souri, Iowa, and Wisconsin. Aggressive pursuit of acquisitions and consolidations is also part of the company's long-term growth plan. Its record of acquisitions and consolidations is as successful as

its original organization and ongoing sales.

In less than four years, United Trust Assurance Company reached the milestone of more than one billion dollars in individual insurance in force. This volume is greater than the volume of more than 70 percent of all life insurance companies in the United States. In addition, whereas it took UTAC less than four years to reach that point, it took an average of 38.1 years for the most recent 25 companies to reach that number. In June 1989 UTAC acquired the Kansas-based Cimarron Life Insurance Company, consolidating Cimarron operations with those in Springfield.

Late in 1987 United Income, Inc., was organized in Ohio as a United Trust affiliate, with almost one-third ownership by the Illinois corporation. Following the United Trust formula, United Income also sold shares based on demographic targeting.

This company set a new record by raising more than $17 million from more than 7,000 investor shareholders—and has subsequently formed United Security Assurance Company (USA), now successfully selling life insurance in Ohio.

By the end of 1990, USA had been selling insurance for only about five months—and had already written more than one million dollars in premiums. In its first full year of marketing, USA wrote more than $4.4 million in premiums.

Stock sales opened in mid-1991 for United Fidelity, Inc. (UFI), the second United Trust, Inc., affiliate. UFI is a holding company in the mort-

gage banking industry, with United Trust, Inc. an equity investor.

Early in 1992 United Trust and United Income combined assets to acquire another holding company, Commonwealth Industries Corporation (CIC). Statutorily the companies have combined assets of approximately $370 million, premium income of about $50 million, and annual revenues of more than $75 million.

CIC, now directly under United Trust Group, controls seven life insurance companies, including Roosevelt National Life Insurance Company, Abraham Lincoln Insurance Co., and Investors Trust Assurance Co. of Illinois; University Guaranty Life Insurance Co. of Ohio; Alliance Life Insurance Co. of Kansas; and Appalachian Life Insurance Co. of West Virginia, in addition to the four United Trust Life companies.

Ryherd, United Trust's chairman and CEO, and Morrow, the company's president and chief operating officer, agree that the original corporate strategy has succeeded in "Building a Midwest company with Midwest people for Midwest people." United Trust, Inc., is publicly traded through the National Association of Securities Dealers

Association Quotation Services (NASDAQ), with about 19 million shares outstanding. United Trust, Inc.'s operating strategy has resulted in successes across the board. There are several key reasons for this.

United Trust, Inc.'s management pays close attention to how corporate assets are invested. This is a key comparison with similar firms across the country. Most of United's assets have always been invested in Triple-A, Double-A, and United States Government bonds, with more than 90 percent in highest quality investment instruments. By

....
Left:
United Trust president and chief operating officer Thomas F. Morrow, left, and chairman and CEO Larry E. Ryherd were among the company's organizers in 1984.
Below:
Pleasant and highly functional modern offices enable the United Trust staff to work in a centralized Springfield location on a wide range of insurance functions.
....

comparison, the top 20 insurance companies in the United States invest an average of 20 percent of their combined assets in non-performing real estate or junk bonds.

Another contributing factor to the company's success is its streamlined approach to administration. For instance, outside of the Columbus-based Ohio office of USA, and the West Virginia office of Appalachian, all operations are consolidated in the Springfield corporate headquarters.

In order to accommodate its growth, the firm has moved twice since it was established. From its first suite of offices, UTI purchased and moved into office facilities at the corner of Second Street and Lawrence Avenue in September 1987. The second move in mid-1992 followed on the heels of acquiring CIC, when UTI moved to CIC's office complex on South Sixth Street. In addition to hundreds of agents in 40 states, about 140 people operate from the Springfield corporate headquarters.

Centralizing the wide range of insurance functions in one spot results in multiple benefits. It eliminates the overhead attached to multiple offices and maintains ready accessibility to corporate records. This, in turn, contributes to the company's track record of low under-

writing expenses. These are front-end expenses, which must be repaid over the life of the policy so the company can profit on the policy. For example, the industry average is $1.58 of expenses to underwrite each dollar of new premium revenue; the UTAC cost was $1.03.

United Trust, Inc., celebrates its successes through the people who make it possible. Photos of those people throughout the state who help the company sell a specific number of contracts are mounted permanently on the Wall of Fame in the headquarters lobby. People who go beyond that milestone are named "President for a Day," with a visit to Springfield as guests of United Trust.

Beyond the company roots, which are firmly planted in Springfield, United Trust, Inc., steadfastly focuses on people in every township and county in the state, routinely invests within the state, and maintains an integral place in the state's agricultural community. The combination of these factors and the targeted market practices have made United Trust, Inc., a one-of-a-kind organization—a Midwest leader.

....
Above:
Product systems support, actuarial claims, reinsurance, underwriting new business, and policy owner service are among the divisions in this United Trust building.
Right:
The serenity of United Trust's lobby is in sharp contrast to the activity which led to the milestone of one billion dollars of individual insurance in force within the company's first four years.
....

First National Bank of Springfield

or 130 years the First National Bank of Springfield has been a forerunner in the banking industry in central Illinois.

Pride in quality service to customers and innovative responsiveness to community growth accounts for First National's historic partnership with the citizens of Springfield. Today, as the last locally owned large bank in Springfield, First National provides an established, well-defined understanding of community and customer needs.

In 1863, shortly after Abraham Lincoln delivered his Gettysburg Address, the National Banking Act authorized the organization of the First National Bank of Springfield by John Williams, a local merchant who became First National's first president. Since then First National has built a solid reputation for customer focus, traditional values, and financial stability.

Today First National is the flagship for Firstbank of Illinois, serving the financial needs of clients throughout the state. First National was chartered as the 52nd national bank of the more than 4,000 banks organized in the United States. In Illinois it is the eighth-largest commercial

bank outside the urban Chicago area, with assets of more than $480 million and primary capital of $40 million.

From its humble beginnings in John Williams' store, First National has grown and prospered along with Springfield and is today considered a leader in our financial community. The bank's home office at Fifth and Adams streets is representative of the company's commitment and support

to the downtown central business district and houses the Commercial Banking departments, Trust and Investment Services, Executive and Administrative offices, and the bank's largest Personal Banking center. Four other full-service retail branches are conveniently located within the city limits of Springfield.

Service is the backbone of this financial institution. The bank and the city of Springfield have fostered a long-term partnership in fulfilling the city's needs for growth, service, quality, and convenience for its citizens. Community involvement, participation, contribution, and staff volunteerism are the cornerstones of this partnership, which has helped build a better community for its people and businesses.

First National Bank provides full-service banking in every sense of the word. The bank shares its expertise on an ongoing basis with customers seeking financial assistance and counseling, based on the belief that banks should be providers of information and education, as well as financial services.

Professional care of all their customer relationships within a framework of efficient and sound banking and trust services will always be a trademark of First National Bank.

Looking to the future, First National celebrates its commitment to the Springfield community with renewed dedication to traditional values and customer-focused service. A strong capital base and professional depth allow First National to provide stable financial services, assistance, and products to create the best opportunities for its individual and corporate customers.

....
Above:
First National's Personal
Banking centers offer
full-service banking
to customers.
Below left:
First National's original
main bank location was
in local merchant John
Williams' store, later moving
to its current accom-
modations at Fifth and
Adams in the heart of
downtown Springfield.
The bank has seen many
changes in 130 years of
business, and continues to be
a symbol of strength and
growth in the community.
....

First of America Bank– Springfield, N.A.

First of America Bank–Springfield is one of the Midwest's largest banks and part of a major regional banking corporation. But it's also as local as a chamber of commerce— a down-to-earth community bank with more than a century-old tradition of quality service and financial stability.

First of America Bank began in 1886 as Illinois National Bank (INB), when it opened its doors at the corner of Fifth and Washington. By the end of its first year of operation, the bank employed six people and had assets of more than $400,000. Its steady growth continued over the years and in 1893 the INB building was erected, becoming Springfield's first skyscraper. In 1972, INB constructed its current facility, then called the INB Center, on the same location. This building,

First of America Center represents the melding of yesterday's heritage with today's progress. Although the building's design is contemporary, it complements the historical character of the Old State Capitol Plaza, which is reflected in First of America Center's bronze glass and polished granite.

which houses other businesses as well as the bank, has brought new life to downtown Springfield while preserving the integrity of the Old State Capitol complex. Today, First of America Bank employs over 400 people and has assets of more than $640 million.

Throughout its history, INB has been a recognized leader in the community and in the economic development of Springfield. Its affiliation with First of America Bank Corporation in 1989, making INB the First of America Bank–Springfield, further solidifies the bank's commitment to the Springfield community. First of America Corporation, one of the top 35 bank holding companies in the United States based on total assets, is ranked in the top 10 for earnings growth and its loan portfolio is consistently rated among the soundest in the industry. In addition, First of America is itself a community bank comprising an extensive network of institutions and branch offices throughout the states of Michigan, Illinois, and Indiana.

Community banking has been the underlying philosophy supporting First of America's stability, growth, and profitability. For First of America, community banking means keeping business and lending decisions close to the customer, pricing products competitively, providing quality service to add value to those products, and reinvesting local deposits within the community. Sharing technology, operating systems, marketing, and training, each First of America affiliate draws upon the resources of one of the Midwest's largest banking companies to address the unique needs of its individual market area.

First of America Corporation and First of America Bank–Springfield put their customers first, through their guiding principles of caring, leadership, quality, and professionalism. Thus, First of America Bank continually offers its customers the industry's best products and services.

This kind of growth is dynamic for the Springfield area. With the construction of new branches, First of America Bank will continue to increase its contribution to local economic development. The number of employees needed at the bank and its branches is steadily increasing; 500 employees are expected to staff First of America's bank locations within the next year.

Bank personnel play a significant role in the community, with involvement in a variety of civic and charitable organizations. The bank encourages its employees to support the United Way and other charitable organizations and aggressively supports the community arts. Bank employees are actively involved in the Springfield Symphony and the Muni

....
The focal point of First of America Center is the interior court where columns of ivy trail down to a reflecting pool. Pyramiding balconies, fronting five levels of offices, rise 70 feet to a glass skylight. The unique environment creates an attractive, professional atmosphere to conduct business.
....

The bank engages in commercial banking, retail banking and mortgage banking, and provides trust and other financial services.

Over the past few years, First of America Bank has grown significantly, doubling its assets. In 1990, the Springfield branch of Germania Bank joined First of America. In October 1991, First of America acquired the Morgan County Community Bank. In July 1992, First of America acquired the First National Bank of Petersburg. First of America Bank now serves Sangamon, Menard, and Morgan counties with seven offices. In 1993, the Champion Federal offices in Springfield, Lincoln, and Taylorville will be added to the bank's branch network, thereby expanding the market area to Logan and Christian counties and increasing the bank's assets to approximately $900 million.

Opera, among others. In 1988, the Springfield Mayor's Award for Significant Contributions to the Arts was given to the First of America Bank, then INB. First of America also strongly supports education through its scholarships, including two, four-year, $10,000 scholarships for local students attending Illinois College and MacMurray College in Jacksonville. Recipients are selected each year for this scholarship.

As the fastest-growing bank in Springfield, First of America promises to continue this rapid growth, bringing more jobs to support the community. Through its unique integration of a national resource base with a sound community-focused, local institution, First of America Bank will remain an economic landmark in central Illinois and the banking industry.

Sorling, Northrup, Hanna, Cullen and Cochran, Ltd.

Sorling, Northrup, Hanna, Cullen and Cochran, Ltd., Springfield's largest law firm, has built its reputation on its responsiveness to the changing legal needs of its clients and the community. As the legal climate has become increasingly more sophisticated, Sorling has successfully continued to meet the varied legal requirements of its clients by growing and becoming more specialized.

Sorling attorneys have joined the firm with backgrounds in banking, accounting, agribusiness,

The firm's extensive law library includes materials on state and federal law, as well as computerized legal research services. The firm has developed customized computer data bases to serve its clients.

government, journalism, nursing, and engineering. The firm meets client needs in specialty areas that include finance, health care, securities, insurance, tax, mergers and acquisitions, real estate, corporate planning, estate planning, public utility regulation, foreclosure law, administrative law, family law, oil and gas law, bankruptcy, labor and employment relations, and eminent domain. Sorling litigation specialists represent both plaintiffs and defendants in civil litigation that encompasses product liability, personal injury, business, com-

mercial and construction litigation, and defense of malpractice claims.

The firm has a long history of involvement in state government. The firm frequently presents client positions before state agencies and commissions, such as the Illinois Commerce Commission and the Human Rights Commission, and legislative committees. The firm counsels clients with regard to legislation and often works with those clients to form or change public policy by assisting in the drafting and shepherding of bills through the legislature. In addition the firm also serves as outside counsel by appointment to several executive agencies. Sorling attorneys have served legislative leaders and political parties. The firm's attorneys have frequently assumed leadership roles in state government, such as chairing the Secretary of State's Advisory Council on Public Records and Privacy.

With its two dozen lawyers and a similar number of paralegals and other support staff, the firm has the resources, experience, and energy to meet major projects head on—from coordinating a multimillion-dollar development to litigating complicated court proceedings. At the same time, the firm continues to satisfy the needs of its individual clients—from planning an estate to handling the purchase of a client's new home.

The Sorling firm is innovative in its approach to client service. The first firm in Springfield to use electronic research, Sorling has embraced state-of-the-art technology, working with its clients to build data bases and develop litigation support systems. As technology has advanced, it has upgraded its own computer systems in order to serve its clients in the most efficient manner possible.

The firm's clients are primarily located in central and downstate Illinois. However, satisfying client needs has led to the development of regional and national relationships. In continuing

client associations that date back 30 years or more, Sorling has followed its clients where their legal demands dictate. In addition to being licensed to practice in Illinois, several Sorling lawyers are also licensed in Missouri; Washington, D.C.; and Arizona.

Carl Sorling launched what would become Sorling, Northrup, Hanna, Cullen and Cochran, Ltd., in 1942. His first partners were John Hardin and B. Lacey Catron, and the firm was first known as Sorling, Catron and Hardin. Charles Northrup, Philip Hanna, George William Cullen, and Thomas Cochran added their names to the firm's early list of lawyers in the 1940s and 1950s and it was their contributions that resulted in a name change to Sorling, Northrup, Hanna, Cullen and Cochran in 1975.

From its earliest days the Sorling firm has played a leading part in the growth and quality of life in the city of Springfield. Its lawyers and staff serve as volunteers and community activists, board and committee members, and officers and trustees of both for-profit and not-for-profit organizations. Sorling lawyers hold or have held leadership positions in the Greater Springfield Chamber of Commerce, the United Way of Sangamon County, the Lions Club, Junior Achievement, the Rotary Club, the Boy Scouts of America, the Urban League, Kiwanis, and Friends of Memorial Medical Center.

Sorling's attorneys are active members of the Sangamon County Bar Association, the Illinois State Bar Association, the American Bar Association, the Illinois Trial Lawyers Association, the American Trial Lawyers Association, the Illinois Appellate Lawyers Association, the Illinois Association of Defense Trial Counsel, the National Health Lawyers Association, the American Agricultural

Law Association, the American Immigration Lawyers Association, and the American Bankruptcy Institute. Several of the firm's lawyers presently serve or have served as officers, board members, or chairmen of the Sangamon County and Illinois State bar associations and the Illinois Trial Lawyers Association.

Sorling lawyers have written articles that have appeared in Illinois Institute for Continuing Legal Education practice handbooks, the *Illinois Bar Journal,* the *Southern Illinois University Law Journal,* the *Illinois Trial Lawyers Journal,* the *Illinois Banker,* and the *Cooperative Extension Service Circular.*

In addition Sorling attorneys have lectured at legal seminars and to civic groups on topics that include taxation, the Uniform Commercial Code, litigation, estate planning, and charitable giving. Some lawyers have also instructed at colleges, universities, and institutes.

Sorling, Northrup, Hanna, Cullen and Cochran, Ltd., has deeply established roots in central Illinois and remains a vital part of the dynamics of the community. All of its lawyers and support staff were either born and reared in the Springfield area or are natives of Illinois. All are committed to Springfield's economy, schools, and quality of life.

Though the firm has changed markedly since the early days of Carl Sorling, Lacey Catron, and John Hardin, its essential goals remain the same—careful attention to the legal needs of the firm's valued clients, both personal and corporate.

....
Above left:
Standing, left to right:
Stephen R. Kaufman, Liesl G. Smith, Michael A. Myers, Michael C. Connelly, C. Clark Germann, Gary A. Brown, Della S. Nelson, David A. Rolf, Craig S. Burkhardt, William R. Enlow, John A. Kauerauf, Fred B. Hoffman, Scott C. Helmholz, Peggy J. Ryan, Mark K. Cullen, Irene H. Gainer, and Thomas H. Wilson. Seated, left to right: Stephen A. Tagge, William S. Hanley, Philip E. Hanna, Charles H. Northrup, Thomas L. Cochran, Patrick V. Reilly, and R. Gerald Barris.
Left:
The firm's offices are located on two floors of the Illinois Building, across from the historic Old State Capitol and Lincoln Law Office in downtown Springfield.
....

Franklin Life Insurance Co.

On a numbingly cold January morning in 1955, several moving vans pulled up in front of the Franklin Life Insurance Company in Springfield with a cargo that would literally revolutionize the business world. As UNIVAC I, the first computer system purchased by a private business, was unloaded, employees stood three and four to a window to watch the huge crane hoist the large computer system up to and through a gigantic hole in the fifth-floor wall.

The tremendous growth increases in Franklin sales and sales associates in the late 1940s and early 1950s created the company's need for increased efficiency and speed, and allowed the company to position itself as a leader in the life insurance industry. Through a unique combination of innovation and conservativism, The Franklin became, and remains, one of the most financially secure life insurance companies in the United States, with more than $30 billion of insurance in force and approximately one million policyowners. Its industry ratings remain consistently high, with the A++ (Superior) rating from A.M. Best, the AAA rating from Duff & Phelps, the Aa2 (Excellent) rating from Moody's, and the AA+ rating from Standard & Poor's.

Springfield is the headquarters for the Franklin, which markets its products and services in 49 states, Puerto Rico, and the U.S. Virgin Islands. In addition, the company has three subsidiaries: American Franklin Life Insurance Co., Franklin Financial Services Corporation, and Franklin United of New York. In 1987, American Brands acquired Franklin Life, keeping the Franklin name intact.

Employees in the home office number more than 1,325, with a field force of more than 3,200 sales associates. An innovative maverick in the 1930s, The Franklin pioneered its Presidential Protective Investment Plan, now called simply the President's Plan. This life insurance program is the company's flagship whole-life plan. Franklin's TAP program offers dual-career, or part-time, opportunites for new sales associates.

The Franklin's commitment to its clients parallels its commitment to its people. Its reputation as "the friendly Franklin" is well deserved and best epitomizes the firm's dedication to building long-term working relationships with its employees and field associates. Franklin has a great tradition of long-term employees—individuals who have devoted an entire career to the organization. With a bimonthly payroll of more than one million dollars, The Franklin's economic impact on the community is significant.

The Franklin's active involvement in community affairs includes support of historic restorations such as that of Lincoln's home, sponsorship of the arts and the theater, participation in community groups and organizations, representation on the Chamber of Commerce board and committees, and contributions to numerous other local events.

Today Franklin's success lies in its commitment to the future, a future which integrates a conservative investment strategy with a progressive outlook and supportive management philosophy that truly are, as the company theme states, "Building Brighter Tomorrows" for clients, employees, and the community.

Above:

Howard Humphrey, chairman, president, and chief executive officer, continues the company's century-old tradition of growth and stability, making the Franklin Life Insurance Company one of the strongest, most financially secure insurance companies in the United States.

Right:

The Franklin philosophy of specialization and unparalleled service, as displayed on this plaque in the home office lobby, is shared equally by the firm's 1,325 employees and its more than 3,200 agency associates in the field.

Andersen Consulting

The computer age has fostered an information explosion, and Andersen Consulting has been there from the beginning. In 1954 Andersen Consulting completed the first successful installation of an electronic computer for a business application. It has since seen technology grow, evolve, and profoundly affect the way organizations do business.

From its earliest days, Andersen Consulting was identified as the consulting arm of Arthur Andersen & Co., which is recognized for its leadership in audit and business advisory, tax, and corporate specialty services. In 1989 the two were designated separate business units with individual operations and managing partners. Today Andersen Consulting is one of the largest management-consulting organizations in the world, and is a leading systems integrator. The Springfield office was opened in 1978.

As a management consultant, Andersen Consulting assists clients in the central Illinois region to create new business strategies, improve operations, and use information technology competitively—among many other services. Clients in the central Illinois area are served by Andersen Consulting professionals from Springfield, St. Louis, and Chicago.

One of the greatest strengths of this regional practice is Andersen Consulting's ability to use its resources and talents not only throughout the state, but worldwide. If needed, client work is enhanced by the entire worldwide network of Andersen Consulting offices, which encompasses more than 21,000 people from 151 offices in 46 countries.

Andersen Consulting distinguishes itself through its scope of services and products, business integration skills, and its ability to serve clients in diverse industries. In central Illinois, the organization's clients are primarily in the government, utilities, manufacturing, health-care, and telecommunications industries.

Systems integration services is a predominant part of Andersen Consulting's business. In systems development projects, Andersen Consulting assumes the role of systems integrator—a prime contractor responsible for selecting and integrating a solution that spans many business functions and often requires the use of multiple vendors.

Beyond systems integration, Andersen Consulting's scope of services includes information and technology planning, systems design and installation, strategic planning, systems management, application software, and CASE (Computer-Aided Systems Engineering) tools.

Andersen Consulting also helps clients "reengineer" or rethink the way they do business in order to improve competitiveness. Business reengineering looks at how all the parts of a company fit together, from strategy to business processes to technology to people. It links information technology to corporate strategy, operational realities, and human resources issues.

Being a business integrator also means offering clients change-management skills that ensure the successful assimilation of technology. Andersen Consulting's change-management professionals help manage and train personnel who are dealing with organizational change.

Andersen Consulting takes pride in its Midwestern roots and strong work ethic. The organization's reputation for competence, professionalism, and client satisfaction has served its clients well for close to 40 years. These elements have proved to be the right mix for success.

The Andersen Consulting partners responsible for the Springfield practice are, from left to right, Steven M. Singer, John J. Warren, and Stephen L. Farmer.

The Horace Mann Companies

With home office staff of about 1,400 people, The Horace Mann Companies represent a major Springfield employer. This giant did not, however, begin as an insurance company, and its first insurance staff totalled three employees occupying a rented second-floor office.

In the 1930s two local teachers, Les Nimmo and Carroll Hall, established the Springfield Teachers Credit Union. Making auto loans to teachers, they realized many auto owners did not have insurance, so the pair organized the Credit Union Interinsurance Exchange. They later approached the Illinois Education Association (IEA) about providing coverage for its members; IEA agreed and IEA Mutual Insurance Company began selling insurance in 1945.

The corporation's three employees made their headquarters in an office on the second floor of the Sangamon County Abstract Company on East Adams. In 1972 a $3-million, six-story home office building consolidated employees who had become scattered among nine Springfield locations.

In 1975 Horace Mann was acquired by the Insurance Company of North America, which later merged with Connecticut General to form CIGNA. Prior to the CIGNA ownership, Paul Kardos was named to the Horace Mann board of directors, becoming chief executive officer in 1982. When Horace Mann was up for sale in 1987, Kardos decided he enjoyed the Horace Mann family spirit, the company's positive nature, and the Midwest so much that he, members of the senior staff, and Gibbons, Green, and van Amerongen (GGVA) bought the company. Then, in 1991, through an initial public offering, the company's stock became available on the New York Stock Exchange. Kardos is an unabashed cheerleader for the Horace Mann Companies. He recounts compliments from the banking community, investment bankers, and insur-

ance departments. "They all think Horace Mann is a quality company. And a quality company comes from quality people," he says. "The Horace Mann vision has not changed...just like in 1945, our mission is to provide financial security to the nation's educators." The company still sees its insurance expertise in the schools, almost 2,600 employees countrywide bring the company's products to the educational community in 47 states. With a portfolio of term and permanent life insurance, group coverage, protection for just about any dwelling called "home," personal property, vehicle, and professional liability insurance, along with annuities and mutual funds, Horace Mann actively plans its future.

A major key to this spirit of forward thinking is the company's "family" organization. Personnel in close-knit divisions work as a family to share information and move toward fulfilling the company's goals.

Through strategic initiatives proposed by research committees, The Horace Mann Companies seeks to expand its market base, serve teachers in new locations and with new coverage, and continue, in the words of Kardos, its "exceptional performance by exceptional people."

The Horace Mann Companies began in Springfield with three employees. Now 2,600 employees bring company products to people in 47 states.

Giffin, Winning, Cohen & Bodewes, P.C.

During the past eight decades, the law firm of Giffin, Winning, Cohen & Bodewes, P.C., has evolved to meet changing needs of Greater Springfield, while retaining a vital interest in government activities.

As 1911 drew to a close, D. Logan Giffin was admitted to the bar and, early the next year, joined legal practice with George Murray. Giffin later joined with Edgar Sampson and, in 1921, the firm of Sampson & Giffin was the first tenant in the newly completed First National Bank Building.

As new members joined the firm, government service continued to be a common interest of many. Giffin, the founding partner of today's firm, was a member of the Sangamon County Board, the Illinois House of Representatives, and the Illinois Senate.

Cornelius J. Doyle served as Illinois Secretary of State and Director of the Illinois Department of Insurance. Montgomery Winning was the First Assistant Illinois General for 24 years, after serving as legal adviser to the Illinois House speaker and as secretary of the Legislative Reference Bureau.

Today's firm is one of the largest in Greater Springfield and focuses on law as it relates to government, real estate development, corporations, businesses, and litigation. Today's partners include

James M. Winning, Robert S. Cohen, Herman G. Bodewes, John L. Swartz, Stephen J.Bochenek, Carol Hansen Fines, R. Mark Mifflin, Thomas P. Schanzle-Haskins, and Gregory K. Harris.

The firm nurtures its Sangamon County niche, declining to open branch offices. Bodewes reflects that the roles of local, state, and federal governments will continue to grow. As a result, businesses and individuals will come to rely more on legal counsel to help them relate to government agencies and regulations. He anticipates Giffin, Winning, Cohen & Bodewes, P.C., will respond to this need.

As it grows, the firm recognizes the need to provide increasingly specialized legal services. Bodewes describes the legal profession as demanding because clients, justifiably, expect prompt and competent service, no matter how specialized it becomes. While recognizing the need for general practitioners in the law profession, the firm acknowledges that specialization is necessary in an era when one individual can no longer be an expert in all legal areas.

Involvement in the community by all members of the firm—in political, philanthropic, religious, business, and social organizations—adds another element of stability to the firm and its future. Traditional legal work, traditional community activities, with changes to meet needs of the Greater Springfield area—it's all a reflection of the tradition that today is Giffin, Winning, Cohen & Bodewes, P.C.

Above: Attorneys in the Business and Government Department of Giffin, Winning, Cohen & Bodewes, P.C., include, standing from left, John L. Swartz and Stephen J. Bochenek; and, seated from left, Robert S. Cohen and Herman G. Bodewes. **Left:** Litigation Department attorneys include, standing from left, Thomas Schanzle-Haskins and Gregory K. Harris; and, seated from left, Carol Hansen Fines and R. Mark Mifflin. The firm traces its Springfield roots back to 1911.

IBM

BM has built its solid and long-standing reputation on providing quality products and services to meet the information systems needs of its customers. This tradition of excellence is fostered throughout IBM's worldwide operations and is the driving force behind its trading area for central Illinois, located in Springfield. As the headquarters for operations, the Springfield IBM facility is closely focused on continually identifying and meeting the diverse needs of its customers, who include both local businesses and governmental agencies.

Since 1941 IBM has operated a marketing branch office in Springfield, offering marketing services and technical support to its customers throughout the area. In 1991 IBM reorganized its branch structure to create a stronger presence in central Illinois. By moving decision-making out into the trading areas, IBM stays closer to its customers and can simultaneously respond quickly.

In addition to trading area headquarters, the Springfield office also houses two separate business units. Each one is uniquely focused to meet the specific needs of the Springfield community. One business unit focuses primarily on state government, forging a growing number of public/private partnerships. This unit provides sales, support, administration, and services tailored specifically to meet the complex hardware, software, and services requirements of agency information systems. As the only national company with this type of concentrated commitment, IBM assists numerous state agencies in maximizing efficiency and productivity through systems-based solutions to performance problems.

A partnership with the Illinois Department of Employment Security (IDES), for example, resulted in the creation of a new business tool, the Image and Records Management system (IRM).

IRM is an automated image system that scans documents and automatically cross-files information for easy retrieval. This system not only manages IDES' millions of forms but also dramatically reduces operating costs and paperwork, thus eliminating tedious, repetitive tasks and increasing performance and productivity.

The second IBM business unit located in Springfield focuses on the private sector and IBM's business partners, who include both customers and suppliers. Through its Business Partnership program, IBM has formed strong alliances with qualified businesses to provide additional support and services to IBM's large base of customers. Such partnerships provide customized products and services for individual customers, both large and small.

IBM is also equally committed to serving the

Right:
The IBM building at 2401 West Jefferson is conveniently located in the northwest section of the city, near the airport, with easy access to the downtown area. This location houses the Mid-American Trading Area headquarters, two marketing offices, service operations, professional services, and product marketing organizations, plus customer executive briefing and classroom facilities.

Below right:
Deb Shultz, team leader, explains some of the finer points of marketing in the public sector to State of Illinois marketing team members Greg Nelson, Alan Burgard, Les Usiak, and Phil DeNotto.

business.

To meet the unique needs of its customers throughout the world, IBM has implemented a strategy called Market-Driven Quality. "Market-driven" at IBM does not mean "marketing driven." Instead, market-driven quality is based on a genuine desire to understand customers' businesses and what they need to be successful. IBM's ultimate goal is total customer satisfaction, and the process of achieving that goal involves continuous adaptation to the rapidly changing demands of the marketplace.

IBM is also committed to the community and its economic, cultural, and social growth. This commitment is reflected in the active involvement of many IBM employees in local civic groups and activities. IBM has, for example, representatives serving on various community boards, including Junior Achievement, Big Brother/Big Sister, United Way, and the Children's Miracle Network Telethon. In addition, the IBM building is often the site for various community meetings and events. Working closely with the Springfield school district, IBM has adopted Hay-Edwards Elementary School. IBM employees donate their time and expertise to work with the school, thus strengthening school/business partnerships in the community.

needs of small businesses, offering a variety of consulting services specifically tailored to the demands of growing businesses.

Client representatives serve as liaisons between IBM and businesses and initiate innovative information solutions to address specific business problems. Systems engineers serve as technical advisors to assist customers in planning for and implementing these solutions. Customer engineers perform installation, regularly scheduled preventative maintenance, and emergency service. Administration assists in the coordination of equipment ordering, delivery, billing, and IBM Credit Corporation financing.

The consulting services aspect of the business is a vibrant and rapidly growing area. The long standing expertise of IBM in the information systems discipline is evolving into services offerings to respond to the changing demands of this dynamic marketplace.

The guided learning center is a self-paced learning center that provides education for IBM users. IBM National Solution Center is an extensive database representing thousands of vendors nationwide. An IBM client representative or authorized agent can use the center to search and select software suited to a specific industry or

IBM's commitment to its three basic beliefs has never wavered: respect for the individual, providing the best customer service possible, and a relentless pursuit of excellence throughout the organization. IBM demonstrates these beliefs to its customers in central Illinois.

....
Above left:
"Practice what you preach."
Claire Cooper, Mid-American
Discovery marketing
representative, teaches Jay
Hocking, systems engineer;
Mike Meisinger, systems
engineer manager; and Kevin
Brobst and Wes Silotti,
systems engineers, the
functions of a new
client/server marketing tool,
TMS/2. This application
downloads data from a large
mainframe nightly and allows
marketing personnel to track
backlogs, do forecasts, and
perform marketing analysis.
Below left:
Dan J. Lautenbach, Mid-
America Trading Area general
manager. Established in
January 1991, the trading
area covers all of central and
southern Illinois and the
easternmost portions of north
Missouri. In October 1991
the greater St. Louis area was
merged.
....

Phillips Brothers Printers

Phillips Brothers Printers opened its doors in 1883 to fill the community's business printing needs. Today they provide publications, newsletters, brochures, and catalogs to commercial businesses, governmental agencies, and to more than 400 colleges and universities nationwide. In fact, most students who attend a college or university probably use a course catalog printed by Phillips Brothers.

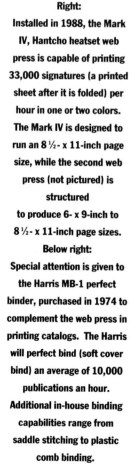

In 1883, when the Phillips Brothers, John and David, founded the firm, the shop was located in downtown Springfield on Fifth Street. Printing custom commercial and Illinois government projects, they quickly established a solid reputation for meeting customer needs with consistent quality printing.

In 1962 Hiram S. Phillips, president and third-generation owner, continued the firm's commitment to quality by acquiring technologically advanced equipment with the change from letterpress to lithographic printing. The growth of the company and the purchase of new equipment led Phillips Brothers in new directions to their present facility at 1555 West Jefferson.

Aggressively seeking new markets, Phillips Brothers identified a niche in the publishing industry and diversified into web printing (a process utilizing roll paper for continuous, long-run book signature printing). In 1974 a perfect binder (used for soft-cover binding) was added to complete the book-printing service, making Phillips a one-of-a-kind printer in Springfield.

In mid-1970, Phillips Brothers took its first step out of the state of Illinois and began contacting colleges and universities across the country. The combination of the web press and perfect

binder was a good match for the course catalogs, producing a quality finished product at an affordable price. This led to Phillips Brothers working with universities from Alaska to Florida.

Major facility expansions in 1988 opened more doors to the future. The firm built an 11,000-square-foot addition to house paper so they could install a second and larger web press. Receptivity to new endeavors and meeting a customer's specific needs remain hallmarks for Phillips Brothers.

Phillips Brothers has shown its commitment to keeping up with changes in technology by attending educational conferences and seminars. These conferences and seminars educate not only the company's management, but also its employees and clientele as changes occur within the printing industry.

A tradition of high quality and competitive pricing has kept customers coming back to Phillips Brothers Printers for more than a century. This tradition, combined with the dedication and loyalty of Phillips' employees, makes the firm's continued success and growth possible.

Right:

Installed in 1988, the Mark IV, Hantcho heatset web press is capable of printing 33,000 signatures (a printed sheet after it is folded) per hour in one or two colors. The Mark IV is designed to run an 8 ½- x 11-inch page size, while the second web press (not pictured) is structured to produce 6- x 9-inch to 8 ½- x 11-inch page sizes.

Below right:

Special attention is given to the Harris MB-1 perfect binder, purchased in 1974 to complement the web press in printing catalogs. The Harris will perfect bind (soft cover bind) an average of 10,000 publications an hour. Additional in-house binding capabilities range from saddle stitching to plastic comb binding.

Springfield Electric Supply Company

"Your connection to quality" is the corporate philosophy behind Springfield Electric, one of the top 100 electrical distribution firms in the United States. Over the past 60 years, this locally owned business has grown from one to eight locations and today represents nearly 200 nationally recognized manufacturers of quality products for industrial, commercial, and residential electrical applications.

The Springfield location also houses a training facility where both associates and customers are educated on new products, applications, and the latest in technological advances. Ongoing technical support is offered to all customers as well.

Thousands of electrical products, from simple wiring devices to sophisticated programmable controllers, are available from all locations for construction, commercial, industrial, institutional, and residential uses. An InterBranch Transfer System links all company branches together through a mainframe computer, making an inventory item in any branch immediately accessible throughout the company.

Continued growth is the forecast for Springfield Electric. A combination of personalized service, efficient order processing, and on-time delivery has built a broad base of loyal, satisfied customers. Quality products at competitive prices are provided by a well-trained, customer-focused staff. A tradition of building long-term, working relationships with suppliers and customers guarantees that Springfield Electric will remain a leader in the electrical-component industry and will continue delivering the superior service its customers have depended on for more than 60 years.

....
Above:
Springfield Electric inventories more than 20,000 items representing nearly 200 leading manufacturers of electrical products. The Springfield Electric Supply Company catalog describes many of the wide range of products that are immediately available from any of the company's eight warehouse locations.
Left:
Located at 718 North Ninth, Springfield Electric supplies a complete line of electrical products to area construction, industrial, commercial, and institutional users. This 42,000-square-foot facility houses the company's corporate offices, supply branch, and warehouse, and the Lighting Center, a full-service residential lighting showroom.
....

Illini Technology, Inc.

Quality, service, and responsiveness to customer needs are the trademarks of Illini Technology, a custom-design electronics manufacturer that has been filling a vital niche in the industrial marketplace since 1983.

Co-founded by John Roth and Mike Jones, Illini Technology offers its customers the latest in electronic manufacturing and assembly processes. A combination of state-of-the-art equipment and a well-trained work force facilitated the firm's 956 percent growth in sales within its first five years, and subsequent listing as a 1989 *Inc.* 500 company.

Illini Technology designs and develops products for a wide range of electronics applications for a variety of industries, including agriculture, automotive, construction, and communications. Through its team of experienced engineers, the company excels in the design and development of analog and digital circuits, microprocessor and computer programming, mechanical design, and electromechanical design.

A firm commitment to continuous quality improvement is part of Illini Technology's culture and corporate strategy. To compete in today's fast-paced, rapidly-changing global marketplace, Illini Technology maintains its competitive edge by continuous improvement of equipment and manufacturing processes. With much of its assembly line processes automated, Illini Technology is also committed to state-of-the-art equipment. Its manufacturing capabilities provide leading-edge technology throughout the manufacturing process, from assembly to testing.

To support its sophisticated production of electronic assemblies, Illini Technology also invests in its people.

Training is a high priority, and close working relationships among its employees and its customers are fostered throughout the company. Its work force of approximately 70 people has both the dedication and the experience to adapt and innovate in order to meet the ever-changing needs of its customers and their industries. Establishing long-term, strategic alliances with its customers enhances Illini Technology's ability to continually meet and exceed their requirements.

With a core of senior assembly and test personnel and a well-trained work force, its central Illinois location is well suited to efficiently produce custom electronic products. With easy access to road and air transportation for delivery of incoming materials and shipment of outgoing products, Illini Technology consistently maintains its customer responsiveness and on-time delivery.

Individualized attention to detail and quality components for customized applications have earned Illini Technology the reputation it holds in the electronics industry. In this age of specialization, Illini Technology proves that competitive manufacturers that do what they do best are uniquely positioned to adapt, innovate, and succeed in the heartland of America.

Above:
Pictured here is an overview of the main assembly area. With a core of senior assembly and test personnel and a well-trained work force, the Springfield location is well suited to serve the marketplace.
Right:
An integral part of the business is the quoting process. John Roth, president (seated), with Mike Jones, vice president/sales and marketing (left), and Cloyce Newton, vice president/engineering (right), reviews documentation prior to submitting a quote to the customer.

Mel-O-Cream Donuts International, Inc.

For 60 years Mel-O-Cream has specialized in donuts—donuts of all kinds—more kinds than they can recall on short notice. The original Mel-O-Cream shop on Jefferson Street, started in 1932 with a $500 investment by Kelly Grant, has seen several changes of direction over the years, but the focus has always been on donuts.

Mel-O-Cream's yeast-raised donuts, still made from a carefully guarded secret formula, are little changed except that potato flour now substitutes for the original mashed potatoes.

Mel-O-Cream started developing a process for freezing yeast-raised dough products in the late 1950s; currently, more than 1.2 million frozen dough pieces produced weekly at their plant are distributed to customers in 11 states.

As a youth, one of the jobs assigned to Mel-O-Cream president, Kelly Grant, Jr., was peeling potatoes for the donuts his dad sold. He formally joined the business in 1953, challenged to build on the reputation established by his father. His brother-in-law, George Warren, purchased an interest in the family business 10 years later, continuing until his death in 1991.

Starting to franchise in the late 1960s, Mel-O-Cream built a new support facility at 800 West North Street. When the franchise operators needed the frozen dough products, the company added a production line capable of supplying 40 franchises; however, high interest rates and a slow economy in 1980-1981 combined to make franchising no longer viable. Making the decision to take their retail-proven products to the newly developing supermarket in-store bakery business, Mel-O-Cream discovered a whole new market.

The frozen dough products produced in Springfield today are the basis for more than 100 varieties after they are thawed, proofed, fried or baked, filled, iced, glazed, and garnished at their ultimate destination. Although new products are added and others dropped, the overall best seller continues to be the original yeast-raised donuts.

The only remaining Mel-O-Cream franchises are in Springfield and Lincoln, Illinois, and are still selling donuts made with the original secret formula.

The company feels that its success in the frozen dough business is due to its concentration on donuts. Also, custom machinery, designed and built in-house, enables successful production of some varieties that could otherwise be made only by hand.

In the pursuit of uniform quality, Mel-O-Cream uses custom-prepared bases to which are added flour, water, yeast, and other necessary ingredients, all carefully weighed and then mixed in high-speed mixers. From working-size pieces, the dough is rolled out into a continuous ribbon of prescribed thickness, cut into desired shapes, frozen, and counted into shipping cases.

While continuing to support its franchised retail shops, Mel-O-Cream's future growth will undoubtedly be in frozen dough production. Toward that end, the company has assembled and is developing a sales, management, and production team capable of substantial new growth.

What would Kelly Grant, Sr., say if he could see his beloved Mel-O-Cream company now?

The management team at Mel-O-Cream Donuts International, Inc., consists of: (left to right) Mark McCloughan, Maintenance Engineering; Tony Bauer, Production Supervisor; David Waltrip, Plant Operations; Dan Alewelt, Assistant Production Supervisor; C. Doug Sweany, Sales; Kelly Grant, Jr., President; Bernice Dale, Office Services; David Ryan, Human Resources/ Distribution; and Jim Eck, Jr., Technical Services.

Frye-Williamson Press, Inc.

Frye-Williamson Press, Inc. can trace its history all the way back to 1836, to Vandalia, then the state capital. Over the years, they've become one of Illinois' leading commercial printers.

It's been a colorful history that includes dozens of memorable projects: all-night runs for last-minute political literature, printing and delivering programs for the New Orleans Mardi Gras, printing secret government documents while armed guards patrolled the plant.

Along the way, Frye-Williamson has consistently maintained its position as a respected industry leader, always in step with the ever-changing printing technology of the twentieth century.

Consider these firsts—all within just 50 years. In 1939 Frye-Williamson installed the area's first 36-inch offset press, which offered unheard of capacity and economy. It was soon followed by the area's first 38-inch, two-color press, and the first two-color perfecting press which prints both sides of a sheet at once. Then, in the early 1980s, Frye-Williamson installed the first of their state-of-the-art, four-color Heidelberg GTO presses.

Today, Frye-Williamson—with 12 operating presses—specializes in four-color printing. But in every sense, the company remains a full-service commercial printer with capabilities that include simple one-color printing, raised-letter printing, typesetting, binding, and die cutting. The technology continues to change, and Frye-Williamson continues to change with it. The current challenge is to deliver high-quality printing that is environmentally friendly—printed on recycled papers, using reformulated inks. Once again, Frye-Williamson is leading the way as these processes become commercially viable.

Frye-Williamson Press, Inc. is owned and operated by Roman Peter Dorr, Jr., and Richard L. Serena.

An artist's rendering of a state-of-the-art, four-color Heidelberg GTO press.

Illinois Association of REALTORS®

The Illinois Association of REALTORS® serves as the "Voice for Real Estate" in Illinois. Founded in 1916, the Association currently has 36,000 members statewide. Since 1948 Springfield has been the headquarters of the Illinois Association of REALTORS®.

All members belong to one or more of the 53 local boards/associations statewide and the National Association of REALTORS®. The term REALTOR® is a registered collective membership mark which identifies a real estate professional who is a member of the National Association of REALTORS® and subscribes to its strict *Code of Ethics*. The *Code of Ethics* is a three-part document addressing the members' responsibilities to the public, the client and customer, and fellow REALTORS® and is enforced through professional standards committees at the local board and state level. In an effort to preserve professional and ethical standards in real estate transactions, the Illinois Association has assisted in the enforcement and improvement of the Illinois statutes for the licensure of real estate brokers and salesmen.

One of the primary missions of the Illinois Association is to protect the rights of private-property owners by recommending and promoting legislation to advance the interest of real-property ownership. At the state level the association monitors some 400 pieces of real estate-related legislation annually. With a decline in the development of affordable housing nationwide, REALTORS® have been instrumental in supporting the creation of state affordable-housing initiatives, including the establishment of the state's first Affordable Housing Trust Fund in 1989. The association also advocates the creation of state real estate finance programs to assist low- and moderate-income buyers, and supports programs to assist first-time homebuyers in achieving the dream of homeownership.

The Illinois Association of REALTORS® (IAR) promotes and fosters educational training for members that increases professional competency. In 1989 IAR was instrumental in the passage of a state law mandating continuing education requirements for real estate licensees and created a voluntary certification of real estate appraisers. The Illinois Association now serves the public as a sponsor for education by offering pre-license, broker, appraisal, continuing education, and professional development training at various times throughout the year.

The Illinois REALTOR® Institute was established in 1964, providing REALTOR® members with an opportunity to earn the Graduate REALTOR® Institute (GRI) professional designation. An individual who earns the GRI designation has voluntarily made a personal commitment to increasing professional service to customers and clients and to obtaining higher levels of education.

REALTOR® members in Illinois are also leaders in promoting fair housing. In 1974 Illinois became the first state in the nation to join with the National Association of REALTORS® to sign the Voluntary Affirmative Marketing Agreement with the U.S. Department of Housing and Urban Development. The agreement ensures the implementation of broad affirmative action, educational, and preventative programs to further promote compliance with fair housing laws.

Across the state, REALTOR® members play an active role in economic development, neighborhood revitalization programs, and other community service programs. The Illinois Association serves as a resource for the institution of these and other programs statewide.

With numerous services and programs provided to members, including regular REALTOR® publications, the Illinois Association of REALTORS® strives to enhance each member's freedom and ability to succeed in business with integrity and competency.

....
Below:
The Illinois REALTORS®
Plaza is located at 3180
Adloff Lane in Springfield.
....

Albanese Development Corporation

he role of a hotel developer/operator begins years before the first traveler arrives, ready to swim in the pool, sleep in a comfortable bed, and enjoy the relaxed surroundings and hospitality. With hotels in six Illinois cities, Albanese Development Corporation (ADC) understands such developments from the ground up.

ADC targets sure-footed growth that carefully considers community needs, market potential, and long-term stability. Company founder Peter Albanese began with modest residential, rental, and commercial developments. These took a back seat, however, after he was invited to develop Medicenter in 1972, now known as St. John's North. Vice president Dennis Albanese explains that the original building was owned by Holiday Inns, Inc., which subsequently introduced the developer to the hotel business.

Soon after Medicenter's completion, Holiday Inns, Inc., encouraged Peter Albanese to purchase the company's existing 254-room hotel in East Peoria. A few years later this was followed by ADC's construction of a new, 198-room Holiday Inn Holidome in Peoria. Although the corporation has since sold those first two Holiday Inns, ADC has built and continues to operate Holiday Inns in Alton, Quincy, and Bloomington (Normal), Illinois. In addition, ADC co-owns and operates the Hampton Inn-Crestwood (Chicago), Illinois.

Albanese Development Corporation properties are generally located near Springfield. Its newest hotel development is a 157-room Hampton Inn adjacent to the Par-A-Dice Riverboat Casino dock in East Peoria.

A local hotel built and operated by ADC is the Springfield Hampton Inn on South Dirksen Parkway.

Albanese Development's overall management

philosophy of total quality is based upon their goal of providing 100 percent guest satisfaction through ensuring excellent service and clean, comfortable surroundings. The Hampton Inn product is designed for the budget-conscious traveler looking for excellent service and accommodations at an affordable price. ADC is committed to its goal of 100 percent guest satisfaction for every stay, Dennis Albanese emphasizes.

Among other local developments are the Trevi Gardens (PUD) subdivision, south of Springfield; Green Meadows Recreation Park, west of the subdivision; and various office buildings, including the Centrum Building medical offices on Madison Street.

The Centrum Building, a multistory structure, includes offices occupied primarily by physicians with specialties that address the area's growing medical needs. Plans call for future expansion north of the Centrum Building to serve and complement the multiple needs of its users.

Peter Albanese explains that the Centrum Complex exemplifies his development philosophy that commercial development is more than dollars and cents. Albanese believes that development requires a thorough knowledge of both the proposed project and the community. It calls for a commitment to serve the market needs through positive community developments, which contribute to economic growth.

Julie Davis, Inc., REALTORS

Julie Davis is keenly aware of numbers, economics, and demographics. These have all contributed to the success of Julie Davis, Inc., REALTORS, and the flagship's associated fleet: Selective Property Services, Inc., the JDR Educational Center, and the property development branch.

Davis, however, insists that what sets the companies apart are five components in the staff's long-term commitment to a common value system:

- **Integrity and Honesty:** "No sale is worth sacrificing our integrity. We want to be legally, ethically, and morally right, with no questions."
- **Community Commitment:** "As a business we benefit from this area's quality of life, and in return our company and our people give back time, talent, and dollars."
- **Marketing:** "In order to get the fairest price in the shortest time, you have to develop a strong marketing program that's right for each property."
- **Continuing Education:** Three program components include training new staff, updating long-term staff on industry-related topics, and offering personal development programs for all.
- **Relocation Programs:** About one new family every business day benefits from the company's wide range of experienced relocation counseling and assistance.

From both a business and a personal perspective, Davis is enthusiastic about Greater Springfield. While the area's stable real estate market does not benefit from inflationary prices, it also avoids disasters during recessions. Government, large institutions, and a cosmopolitan atmosphere blend with a small-town familiarity and family-oriented environment where it's easy to become involved.

The firm's services benefit both Springfield and other area towns. Julie Davis, Inc., REALTORS, lists residential, commercial, and agribusiness properties. Selective Property Service, Inc., manages residential, commercial, and condominium properties. JDR Educational Center offers courses for prelicensing of salespeople and brokers as well as continuing education for agents. Julie Davis, Inc., REALTORS, also develops residential subdivisions, office buildings, and condominiums.

In addition to heading the companies' local activities, Davis is a senior instructor for the REALTORS National Marketing Institute. Through this educational affiliate of the National Association of REALTORS, she receives nationwide exposure to business owners and their proven business ideas.

Since establishing the business in 1979, Davis has emphasized a commitment to serve all people. "Our agents come from all walks of life, live in all areas, and are involved in all sorts of activities," she explains. "Springfield is a great place to live and we want to be here 20 years from now, growing and changing to meet the needs of all people."

....
Above:
Julie Davis, owner of Julie Davis, Inc., REALTORS, is enthusiastic about Greater Springfield. She looks forward to meeting the area's changing needs that result from future growth.
Left:
The office of Julie Davis, Inc. REALTORS, also houses associated companies. These include Selective Property Services, the JDR Educational Center, and the property development branch.
....

Lincoln Land Development Company

Economic development for Springfield and the surrounding area has been the cornerstone of Lincoln Land Development Company, a Springfield-based firm with extensive experience in the successful completion of both commercial and residential developments since 1956. That's why Leonard W. Sapp, president of Lincoln Land Development Company and founder and chairman of the board of Leonard W. Sapp & Associates, Inc., has been called the "imagineer." His foresight, as well as his insight, created the vision for numerous developments throughout the area, including Parkway Pointe, Fairhills Mall, Sangamon Center North, and the Rail Golf Course and its residential development—just to name a few.

Returning home to Springfield from the navy in 1945, Leonard Sapp formed a partnership with James Brunk to operate Brunk and Sapp. This retail business sold farm equipment, saddlery goods, hardware, and appliances and reflected its owners' mutual hobby as well—raising Shetland ponies, which were in high demand at the time. Traveling around the country, showing ponies, and selling livery goods from their trailer met both business and leisure goals for the two entrepreneurs, until the demand for ponies declined suddenly around 1954.

What started out as a dilemma for Sapp—what to do with more than 100 ponies—became the impetus for Lincoln Land Development Company. On a Sunday afternoon in 1955, Leonard Sapp and his wife, Lovene, offered a free pony with every lot purchased in their first subdivision,

Val-E-Vue Acres. They sold 59 lots in the next 60 days. Lincoln Land Development Company was formed, and by 1957 Sapp was buying more ponies to keep up with the demand for his lots.

Throughout the 1950s and 1960s, Lincoln Land Development developed subdivisions and built apartments and single-family homes throughout Springfield and Sangamon County. In 1970 the firm entered the commercial market with Fairhills Shopping Center, the first enclosed mall in Springfield. Sangamon Center North, Illinois Realtors Plaza, Oak Terrace Active Retirement Community and Healthcare Center, and the Rail Golf Course, among others, followed. Eventually commercial developments became the mainstay of the business.

Today the company develops and

manages commercial properties throughout the Springfield area. From site selection to project design and quality construction, Lincoln Land Development builds properties uniquely designed to meet the specific needs of its individual clients. The firm also specializes in commercial real estate, development, leasing, and management of investment properties. Applying high standards in property management, including innovative preventative maintenance, Lincoln Land Development coordinates and works with a variety of individual clients and other commercial brokers.

Projects in recent years include the 174-acre, multiuse business development known as Parkway Pointe, located south of White Oaks Mall on Veterans Parkway. Comprising retail stores, office buildings, hotels, food service, and light manufacturers, Parkway Pointe illustrates the economic impact Lincoln Land Development Company has had on the Springfield area. As stated in a report prepared by the Economic Development Council of the Greater Springfield Chamber of Commerce: "Parkway Pointe represents a rare opportunity for Springfield to generate a large number of new jobs, tax revenues, and consumer income. It will also provide the community with a modern industrial park to accommodate new business and will ensure retention of an important existing industry."

Other planned projects include Prairie Crossing, a 128-acre project southeast of Parkway Pointe comprising office space and commercial businesses, including restaurants and hotels; Southwest Gardens, which includes apartment space and retail business outlets.

Lincoln Land Development helps the community, as well as the economy, grow. Working closely with the City of Springfield, the Greater Springfield Chamber of Commerce, local businesses, and other community leaders, the firm identifies improvement and development needs and thoughtfully researches opportunities to meet those needs. Once a project is determined to be feasible and resources are carefully aligned, Lincoln Land Development manages and leads development. Its goal is to manage effectively and to lead effectively.

Helping the Springfield area grow, creating more jobs, and implementing innovative ideas are Lincoln Land Development's overriding corporate objectives. In one 18-month span, for example, Lincoln Land Development Company created more than 1,200 new permanent jobs and brought a number of new businesses to Springfield, improving the quality of life and work for central Illinois residents.

Over the years Leonard W. Sapp & Associates and Lincoln Land Development Company have developed hundreds of living units and more than 800,000 square feet of office and commercial space. Covering every aspect of the real estate profession, Lincoln Land Development is considered one of the most efficient and prestigious firms in central Illinois.

Left:
This 18-hole, championship golf course was designed by Robert Trent Jones. The course hosts the LPGA Rail Charity Golf Classic each Labor Day weekend. The purse has grown from $50,000 in 1976 to $450,000 in 1992. More than $530,000 has been donated to statewide charities during the 16 years of the tournament.
Below Left:
The Parkway Pointe development, a 174-acre tract of land on Springfield's southwest side, has created more than 2,000 permanent jobs and now produces more than $130 million in annual sales, which provides a real estate and sales tax basis that helps bolster the economy of Springfield.

Sankey Construction, Inc.

Before traffic can roll down the new highway, before the airplanes can touch down at the expanded airport, before the first car can park in the new lot— Sankey Construction, Inc. may have already been there.

Sankey Construction, Inc., equipment is a familiar sight wherever Greater Springfield grows. Specializing in heavy and highway construction, site preparation, airport runways, subdivision and industrial site development, street projects of all sizes and the storm and sanitary sewer line installations which frequently accompany these projects.

Established in 1948 as Sankey Brothers, Inc., an asphalt paving company, the company now completes concrete paving as well. The original company was purchased in 1986 by Kenneth E. Newton and John A. Mifflin. The new owners changed part of the name enough to reflect the new organization, while retaining that portion which reflects the firm's heritage and experience.

Sankey Construction features a professional and technical staff to back up the construction personnel. It is the only heavy construction company in town with five engineers and four engineering technicians on its full-time staff. During the height of a busy summer construction season, more than 250 additional employees are also on the payroll.

Headquarters for this major construction firm are located on 17 acres of land just northeast of the Clearlake Avenue overpass. The site is home to an asphalt plant, repair yard, equipment storage area and materials handling yard.

The quality of their work is reflected in the awards the company has earned from their peers. In 1987, Sankey Construction was named by the Illinois Department of Transportation as the state's Outstanding Bridge and Paving Contractor. The same year, the firm was nominated as the Outstanding Asphalt Contractor. A national Proof of Quality Award was presented in 1988 by the National Asphalt Pavement Association.

Sankey Construction, Inc. is a member of the Illinois Asphalt Pavement Association, National Asphalt Pavement Association, Associated General Contractors of Illinois and Associated General Contractors of America. The company has also been involved locally with the organization and support of Build Sangamon County. This association of contractors, equipment dealers, material suppliers, labor groups and financial institutions focuses on projects which are key to the infrastructure of Sangamon County.

Sankey Construction, Inc.—innovative, flexible, experienced—and a familiar sight wherever there is growth in the Greater Springfield area.

Goodwin & Broms, Inc.

"A better solution is the most important thing we offer," says Daniel Goodwin, a principal of the consulting engineering firm of Goodwin & Broms, Inc. In their specialty of environmental engineering, a better solution can be offering a lot.

The firm specializes in the areas of environmental regulation, pollution control, and waste management. This work may include such wide-ranging assignments as advising on regulatory compliance, preparing reports or permit applications for EPA, monitoring wastewater discharge, investigating leaking underground storage tanks, or evaluating commercial properties for environmental hazards prior to sale.

Goodwin and Robert Broms both worked for the Illinois Environmental Protection Agency, and later formed independent consulting practices before merging their businesses in April 1989. They projected growing to a staff of ten employees within three years. By April 1992, however, their staff totalled 18, an additional office had been established in Davenport, Iowa, and plans for construction of a new office building in Springfield were near completion.

A major segment of the firm's work involves underground storage tanks, which can cause significant concerns when they leak. "Right now there are no cheap and easy ways to clean up the problems," Goodwin admits, although he describes a Goodwin & Broms approach.

Many leaks occur at abandoned or operating gas stations. Contaminated soil must be removed so that contaminants do not, for instance, seep into groundwater. Commonly the removed soil is buried at a landfill where it is not decontaminated and cannot be reused.

Goodwin & Broms may recommend an approach in which contaminated soil is treated biologically or in special thermal treatment equipment to remove the contaminants. After treatment, that soil can be used as fill for another site.

This approach is often "more economical, avoids risks to the client, and it gets the job done," Goodwin explains.

Goodwin & Broms, Inc., clients include *Fortune* 500 corporations and family-owned businesses, as well as occasional citizens groups. The

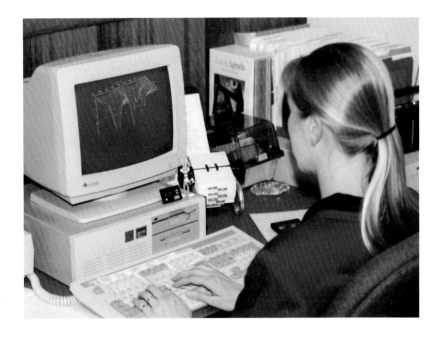

company differentiates itself in several ways from similar consultants. Its Springfield location provides convenient access to regulatory agencies. Long-term experience of the principals in the Water Pollution and Air Pollution Divisions of EPA results in understanding how those divisions function and provides ongoing professional relationships with agency staffs.

Goodwin stresses that the firm is not radically environmentalist. Instead, he explains, "We see Goodwin & Broms as a viable means of serving the needs of our community, state, and nation; to change those past practices that have caused today's environmental problems and to move society in the direction it has to go, without being disruptive or frittering away our limited financial resources on poor ideas for environmental protection."

A Goodwin & Broms geologist uses a computer model to simulate the spread of groundwater contamination resulting from a leaking underground storage tank.

LEXIS Document Services

L EXIS Document Services (LDS) is a "shining gem" in the Springfield business community. Since its founding as Illinois Code Company in 1962 by Donald and Betty Timm, the firm has continued its dedicated commitment to meeting the public record-searching and -filing needs of the financial and legal communities.

LEXIS Document Services helps individuals, businesses, and corporations of all types and sizes locate, retrieve, and file public documentation. With three decades of experience in document filing and searching, LDS assures its more than 5,000 customers prompt access to state and county records, both nationwide and outside the United States. Its customer base includes the nation's leading banks and top law firms.

Its extensive service network offers access to a variety of public documents, including Uniform Commercial Code financial statements; Secretary of State incorporation files, such as good-standing certificates and articles of incorporation; tax liens, judgments, and pending lawsuits; Securities and Exchange Commission documents; and trademarks, patents, titles, court cases, and other public records. Since its purchase by Mead Data

Central, Inc., a leader in electronic database publishing and a division of the paper producer, Mead Corporation, the Illinois Code Company has been doing business as LEXIS Document Services.

LDS has developed an extensive nationwide network of agents and correspondents to file or obtain copies of documents kept in any state, county, or other municipal government office in the United States. All acquisitions, business expansions, and mergers require document services.

Quality, reliability, and responsiveness are LDS trademarks. Expertise in different filing and search requirements provides LDS with the flexibility to meet customer needs quickly and accurately. Many requests are confirmed by phone the same day, followed up by a written report containing copies of the retrieved documents upon release by the government agency. Personal attention to individual requests is what makes LDS unique.

High-quality service and a staff dedicated to meeting the customer's needs makes LDS a true "gem" in the Springfield marketplace.

Right:
The hard-working staff at LEXIS is dedicated to responsiveness to customers' needs.
Below:
Quality, reliability, and responsiveness are LEXIS trademarks.

Alice Campbell Temporaries, Inc.

"**N**obody told me I shouldn't start the way I did," Alice Campbell reflects today. In 1981 she was looking for a challenge and had a dab of money and an office with a typewriter and a telephone. From those modest beginnings, when Alice admits she was "scared to death," has grown Alice Campbell Temporaries, Inc., proud to boast it is "Springfield Born/Springfield Owned/Springfield Managed."

During the company's early days, Alice wrote resumes to pay the rent. She estimated that without a word processor and with only moderate typing skills, she produced dozens of retyped pages. Her passion for doing a job to meet client requirements has been a guiding force ever since.

Temporary employment goes far beyond placing only office staff, Alice explains. One of the business' most unusual matches was the man who carved names on tombstones. "We never found him another job he liked as well," she says. There have been other unusual placements, too—artists, a doctors' seminar coordinator, and an editor for a book on pacemakers. Alice Campbell Temporaries and the affiliated corporation in Tucson, Arizona, believe "every customer is unique," and customer service is their reason for being in business. Whatever the placement, prospective temporaries receive thorough skill evaluations, counseling, and training so that they are prepared for future placements. Each temporary is matched with an employer's specific needs in terms of talents, background, time commitment, and personality.

The company identifies trends and changes in the temporary service industry through its membership in the Temporary Independent Professional Society. This nationwide organization screens prospective members carefully and meets twice a year to exchange information on such wide-ranging topics as marketing, reference forms, and evaluation strategies. Since there is no competition among members, everyone benefits from their shared successes.

A growing, nationwide trend is that of executive or professional placements. If the need develops in the Greater Springfield area, Alice foresees establishing a division to fill temporary corporate staffing positions.

Premier Temps is a program initiated several years ago at Alice Campbell Temporaries, Inc. The people who earn this designation are "an integral part of the staff" where they are placed. While flexibility for both the temporary and the office is retained, a more long-term relationship is established.

An important company goal is to make each temporary feel a part of a cohesive work force. This can be difficult, Alice admits, when dozens of individuals work in dozens of locations. Consequently, employees focus on companywide activities such as taking part in community fund-raisers.

A supporter of Greater Springfield and loyal to the firm's temporaries, Alice sums up the company's philosophy simply: "We try to attract the best work force for our great clients."

Above:
Alice Campbell,
president and owner.
Seated: Judy Huston,
administrative vice
president.
Below left:
Standing left to right:
Mary Snyder, Carlinville
Manager; Phyllis Suiter,
customer service
director; and Linda Smith,
financial director.

Holiday Inn East Hotel and Conference Center

The Holiday Inn East Hotel and Conference Center, throughout its 30 years in Springfield, has consistently been regarded as a leader in stable management, superior accommodations, and gracious service for corporate travellers, conventioneers, and individual families visiting the capital city. The hotel is host to an ever-changing variety of clientele. From the elegance of the annual Springfield Art Association Ball to 50 fire engines with 130-foot ladders to million-dollar Arabian horse auctions, the Holiday Inn East offers a flexible, exciting, and professional environment.

The hotel, a 380-room property, is situated on 26 acres off Interstate 55 on Dirksen Parkway. It is the most popular and versatile hotel in Springfield and central Illinois. This is evident by the fact that it consistently runs the highest occupancy of any major hotel in the city. Of its convention and meeting business, 19 groups have been returning annually for more than 10 years.

The principal features, a 13,000-foot ballroom and the 35,000-square-foot Holidome, create an exceptional facility. The Presidential Ballroom can accommodate up to 1,800 people for a meeting, or 1,400 for a banquet. The ballroom can also be divided into seven separate meeting rooms, all in proximity to one another.

Unique to central Illinois is the hotel's Audio/Visual Theatre, which provides a multi-

media atmosphere for educational, entertainment, or informational events. The theatre has plush, graduated seating and a complete array of the latest state-of-the-art audio/visual equipment.

The Executive Boardroom incorporates high-tech planning with ergonomic comfort. The design of the conference table, chairs, and specialized lighting, with color-corrected lamps and non-glare lenses, promotes a comfortable and productive work environment. For many groups these two rooms demonstrate the hotel's commitment to providing guests with the best in meeting facilities.

The Holiday Inn East features a variety of dining facilities. The Terrace Dining Room offers a wonderful prime rib buffet. Many guests comment that it is the best-kept secret in town on Saturday evenings. Casual dining is provided by the Green Tree Cafe. The Galaxy Lounge presents live entertainment nightly, except Sunday.

The Holiday Inn gift shop attracts many hotel guests. Besides its stock of basic necessities, the shop carries the latest in fashion, exquisite gifts, and a wide assortment of souvenirs.

The 35,000-square-foot Holidome is a year-

Above:

The Holiday Inn East Hotel has been recognized as the leader in the hospitality industry in Springfield. In 1991 more than 73 percent of their group business was repeat customers. Each year for more than 10 years, 19 groups have returned.

Right:

The 35,000-square-foot Holidome is as large as a football field. Everyone enjoys the year-round, indoor recreation center. In addition to the pool, the Holidome includes an exercise room, putting green, whirlpool, and arcade.

the Raynor Hotel Corporation, a subsidiary of Raynor Garage Doors, has been the sole owner of the hotel. Ray Neiswander, Jr., the current president, and Esther Lausen, chief executive officer of the Raynor Hotel Corporation, continually update and improve the individual amenities in each guest room, the public meeting rooms, and restaurants. Proof of their commitment to excellence is the recently announced, four-year renovation and new construction project that will assure the hotel's continued success and solidify its position as a leader in quality accommodations and guest satisfaction in Springfield and central Illinois.

In compliance with the American Disabilities Act standards, the redesigning of 12 guest rooms for accessibility has been completed. Site preparation for future enhancement will be finished in 1992. Construction of the new facilities will begin in 1993. Emphasis will be placed on upgrading mechanical and electrical services, improving housekeeping and laundry areas, increased meeting space, and providing exquisite recreation amenities. The goal of the owner and management team is to have a hotel designed that will not only be a signature property for all Holiday Inns, but will also be regarded with esteem throughout the hospitality industry.

round, indoor recreation area. The indoor pool, sauna, Jacuzzi, shuffleboard, putting green, arcade, and playground are all situated in a beautiful tropical garden setting. The Holidome's banquet space is extremely popular for picturesque weddings, Hawaiian luaus, and numerous political and social receptions.

The Oasis Snack Bar, the hotel's third food outlet, is located in the center of the Holidome, easily visible to guests when they're enjoying the recreational amenities. This restaurant offers an economical alternative for families and student groups touring Springfield. Guests often return to enjoy the best cheeseburgers and nachos in town.

The Holiday Inn East has been awarded the Superior Hotel Award for four consecutive years based on its quality facilities and its greatest asset—the caring and helpful staff. This award is presented to only the top 10 percent of all 1,600 Holiday Inns worldwide. A hotel is selected and critiqued on quality, service, guest satisfaction, and property appearance. The housekeeping staff also received the 1990 Gleam Team award presented by Holiday Inn, Inc., (they finished second in 1989). This award is based on room appearance, the lost and found system, and response time of maids and maintenance staff. Under the direction of its founder, Ray Neiswander, Sr.,

Left:
The Oasis Snack Bar offers an economical alternative to both student tour groups and families touring Springfield. It is located in the center of the Holidome and is easily visible to guests who are enjoying the recreational activities.
Below:
The Audio/Visual Theatre is the hotel's most unique meeting room. It provides a professional atmosphere for groups of up to 108. A full array of audio/visual equipment and a rear-screen projection system are featured. With this environment many planners comment that their attendees are less distracted and can absorb information more easily when their seminars are held in the Audio/Visual Theatre.

White Oaks Mall

When White Oaks Mall held its grand opening in August 1977, most Springfield residents could only begin to imagine the many ways this super regional shopping center would contribute to the city and to central Illinois.

When planning began for the one-million-square-foot shopping center, most Springfield-area residents did not share the vision of the Barker and Lubin families, and Melvin Simon & Associates, the owner-developers. Conventional wisdom said that people wanted convenient shopping. Conventional wisdom said White Oaks' location beyond the western fringe of Springfield did not provide convenience.

White Oaks Mall became, however, a stimulus for subsequent westside Springfield developments. The 65-acre mall site is home for 125 stores, with parking for 4,700 cars. What began as a center outside the Springfield city limits now sits as the hub of several shopping clusters.

Malls today reflect changes in society. When families began moving to the suburbs, malls followed, providing convenient shopping and recreation. Today's families have less time to spend together—and many families spend their joint time shopping.

The team at White Oaks Mall has responded by creating a family place with a mix of unique activities that contribute to a sense of community and citizenship. More than just a shopping center, White Oaks Mall is seen as a community center and a good neighbor.

It is open at the crack of dawn for mall walkers to enjoy this healthy activity in a climate-controlled atmosphere before the stores open. Mall activities appeal to a variety of interests, including fashion, cars, sports, crafts, antiques, even television personalities for adults and superheroes for children.

Visits to Santa Claus and the Easter Bunny at White Oaks have become part of family traditions. Parents know they can enjoy a Halloween costume contest and safe trick-or-treating every year. These family-oriented activities and fond memories have developed the feeling that this shopping center belongs to everyone.

Special events for the family are just one component of the overall contributions made by White Oaks Mall to the Springfield community. Additional contributions are, of course, economic. The city benefits from the infusion of sales and property taxes generated by the mall, as well as from the part- and full-time employment opportunities for more than 3,000 people.

The primary purpose of White Oaks Mall is shopping. The mall has something for everyone, with an attractive mix of local, regional, and national tenants. Because successful merchants are the key to any shopping center, the mall team works closely with its merchants to build their

more than 90 minutes per visit, twice the national average.

White Oaks acted as a cornerstone for economic development in southwest Springfield. Subsequent growth of nearby shopping areas now brings traffic to White Oaks from customers who may not have originally considered the mall as a destination. Growth and shopping habits are supported by Springfield's existing employment mix, which provides a certain resistance to recession.

business and promote growth. Entrepreneurs can work with White Oaks Mall's Retail Development Program to develop new concepts for specialty retailing. Many entrepreneurs display their goods on a seasonal basis.

As part of what is a natural growth cycle in the retail industry, White Oaks Mall is maturing. While other malls of a similar age are experiencing a leveling of their traffic counts, White Oaks continues to grow and prosper. Drawing from a 10-county trade area, the mall consistently records 10 percent increases in the number of shoppers visiting the center. Statistics also show that each of the eight million shoppers at White Oaks Mall spend

Opportunities to meet the evolving needs of the community, customers, and merchants make change another constant at White Oaks Mall. The mix of retailers will change. The mall's look will change. Shoppers' reasons to visit White Oaks will change as they mature from childhood, through adolescence, and into adulthood.

But long into the next century, shoppers will continue to anticipate the mall's seasonal excitement. They will treasure the memories of shopping at White Oaks for the special occasions of their lives. And central Illinois residents will continue to think of White Oaks Mall as their good neighbor.

Above Left:
Team members from White Oaks Mall annually transform Center Court and the broad walkways into a magical holiday wonderland.
Left:
Every year, children proclaim decisively that "the real Santa" sets up his Springfield headquarters at White Oaks Mall.

Springfield Renaissance Hotel

I n a Midwestern city that claims ties to some of America's most famous figures resides an elegant, 4-Diamond hotel that has inspired a history of its own.

Springfield, Illinois, in the heart of the Midwest's plentiful cornbelt, is home of Abraham Lincoln, Vachel Lindsay, and the current seat of state government. Springfield is also the home of the Springfield Renaissance Hotel, an impressive, 11-story, red brick structure in the heart of downtown. Today, in this tourist-filled city, it is the only local hotel with a direct, underground connection to the newly built Prairie Capital Convention Center.

Nestled in the heart of Springfield's historic downtown district, the Renaissance is within walking distance of several famous Lincoln sites. Just two blocks south of the hotel lies Abraham Lincoln's home. Operated by the National Park Service, the home has been totally refurbished, and tours are free to the public. Just one block east of the home is the historic Great Western Depot, where Lincoln gave his farewell address upon leaving Springfield for Washington.

The Lincoln-Herndon Law Office and the Illinois Old State Capitol, where Lincoln worked as a young attorney and later, as an Illinois statesman, are just another two blocks west of the Renaissance Hotel. Not too far away, on the north edge of the city, Abraham Lincoln's tomb stands in Calvary Cemetery, a national landmark that attracts hundreds of thousands of visitors each year.

In addition to its awards, prestigious location, and impressive facade, the Renaissance Hotel has always meant elegant accommodations for tourists, business travelers, and convention and meeting attendees. It has become the favorite hotel of superstars and famous

political figures when visiting Springfield. The Renaissance Hotel has become the first choice among those who want "big city" accommodations but the flavor of a small Midwestern town.

Among the Renaissance Hotel's basic guest amenities are complimentary valet drop-off and parking under a spacious, all-weather canopy. Arriving guests traverse a polished marble floor that runs the entire length of the lobby. The lobby area has been constructed from fine mahogany woods, burgundy and pastel carpets, and original antique furnishings, illuminated by recessed lighting and porcelain lamps. It is a breathtaking yet comfortable environment.

This same atmosphere extends throughout the hotel's fine restaurants, prefunction area and elegant meeting rooms, and suites. The Renaissance Hotel boasts the only complete concierge service, an amenity not yet adopted by any other chain in the city. With the help of the hotel's concierge staff, guests can book dinner reservations and rent cars, computers, cellular phones, and more. The Renaissance concierge staff can also help guests plan walking tours of the city, arrange

Right:
Abraham Lincoln's home is located just two blocks from the Renaissance Hotel.
Below:
The Springfield Renaissance Hotel is located in the heart of Springfield's historic downtown district.

hotel boardinghouse as well as a local pub for the city's high society. At dusk the Globe Tavern turns into a favorite after-work spot for a quiet cocktail and complimentary hors d'oeuvres. For dinner Lindsay's again provides a comfortable setting for everything from a family meal to an elegant supper for two.

Guests and residents also flock to Springfield's true gourmet dining establishment, Floreale. This wonderfully inviting dinner restaurant is located within the Renaissance Hotel and features the Nouvelle style of French culinary arts, under the direction of executive chef Stephen Cummings, a native of Manchester, England. To the casual observer, Floreale's dark ambiance, hand-blown Venetian chandeliers, and wall sconces may seem a bit intimidating. But the friendliness of the room's staff is a true delight, ensuring the comfort of each guest. Of course, a true gourmet would find Floreale exceptional also. The menu in Floreale changes often, assuring a wide variety of entrees to repeat customers and keeping cooking talents sharp.

The Springfield Renaissance Hotel will continue to provide history buffs as well as business-minded travelers with the unmatched quality of service and luxurious accommodations that it has provided over the years. Its reputation as the finest hotel in downstate Illinois will stand for many years to come.

....
Left:
Springfield's finest dining room, Floreale, features elegant surroundings and a unique dining experience.
Below:
The Renaissance Health Club features sauna, whirlpool, weight room, and indoor pool.
....

carriage sight-seeing trips, make recommendations on local entertainment options, and supply baby-sitting services.

All of the hotel's 316 guest rooms are carefully furnished and decorated to carry the same comfortable atmosphere found throughout the hotel. Dark woods, burgundy carpets, and pastel room linens are tastefully mixed with the latest in-room amenities, including individual coffeemakers, an in-room bar, hairdryers, remote-control television, even bottled water.

Each morning, guests can choose to exercise in the hotel's indoor health club and swimming pool or partake of a hearty breakfast in the friendly atmosphere of Lindsay's restaurant, which serves as the hotel's all-day dining outlet. Lindsay's Restaurant, named for native poet Vachel Lindsay, is adorned with replica artwork and inscribed poetry from the famous poet and painter.

Lindsay's offers a complete breakfast buffet and delicious menu items, including a special "calorie counter" menu. For lunch, Lindsay's offers a spectacular buffet of soups, salads, and meats, plus a huge variety of luncheon menu favorites. The Globe Tavern, with its inviting dark woods and forest-green furnishings, features a walk-around bar, two large-screen televisions, and plenty of comfortable seating. Wall hangings depict the history of the Globe Tavern, dating back to the mid 1800s. The original Globe Tavern was once Abe and Mary Todd Lincoln's first home; back then the Globe was somewhat of a

Springfield Convention and Visitors Bureau

With Springfield as the state capital and Abraham Lincoln's "hometown," the Springfield Convention and Visitors Bureau (SCVB) markets Illinois' leading downstate tourism city. The bureau works for the community, getting Springfield's share of travel dollars by creating awareness and recognition of the city's attractions.

In any tourism city, travelers support restaurants, stores, attractions, and hotels and also ride in taxis and buses. Salaries are paid to employees of these entities, and those employees, in turn, support the local economy and live in the area.

More than one million dollars in sales and use taxes are paid by tourists annually, which directly contributes to the Springfield community. Thus more jobs are created and Springfield's general commerce is improved. The SCVB is funded by the hotel/motel tax, not by property taxes, so tourism marketing money is created by the visitors.

Three groups are SCVB's target markets. The first group comprises the leisure market, or people taking pleasure trips. The SCVB reaches this market by advertising in regional and national publications, mailing and distributing brochures in response to visitors' inquiries working with the travel media.

SCVB's second market is the group market. More than 100,000 students come to Springfield annually, bringing more than two million dollars to the local economy. According to the National Tour Association, the impact of adult motorcoach tours to Springfield is more than three million dollars.

Conventions and meetings are the focus of the SCVB's third market. Prospective associations, corporations, and organizations considering holding a convention or meeting in Springfield are contacted via telemarketing, sales calls, and participation in national trade shows. The SCVB is constantly looking for new organizations that could meet in

Springfield. Retaining current business is another focus. Once a group is booked into Springfield, the SCVB works to ensure a successful meeting by offering a variety of free services, including registration assistance and program planning.

Visitors come from all over the nation and the world. As an accessible drive-in destination, the city draws the bulk of its visitors from Illinois and surrounding states. In addition, approximately 100 countries a year are represented by international visitors.

The State Capitol and Lincoln attractions are only part of Springfield's tourism success. The Carillon in Washington Park is one of the largest in the world. One of Frank Lloyd Wright's most famous buildings is just blocks from downtown Springfield. The Henson Robinson Zoo, Lincoln Memorial Garden, and Lincoln's New Salem are nearby.

The SCVB works closely with the Springfield Park District, the State Bureau of Tourism, the Historic Preservation Agency, and the State Museum to ensure that all events or sites are marketed to their fullest.

While the SCVB consists of a staff of 13 full-time, 12 part-time convention personnel, and seasonal employees, they also rely on the help of many volunteers who assist at events and at sites. Outside of Chicago, the SCVB is the largest convention visitors bureau in Illinois. With all it has to offer, it's no wonder Springfield is one of the leaders in Illinois' tourism industry.

....
Above:
Tourism is a major factor
in Springfield's economy.
Right:
Class trips to Springfield
bring an estimated 100,000
students to Springfield
annually.
....

Paris Fabricare Specialist, Inc.

Paris Fabricare co-founder Frank Franke once observed, "You can go to the bank and borrow money, but you can't go and borrow some good reputation. Therefore, along with your daily business deposits, deposit a small amount of good reputation in your personal account. No one can give it to you and no one can take it away."

Paris Cleaning Company was established in 1909 by this German immigrant tailor and his eldest son, Carl D. Franke, Sr. Originally located at 313 East Monroe, the cleaners took its name from Paris, France, where chemical cleaning began. Chemical cleaning was revolutionary, but successful, and in 1913 the operation moved to the Coats Watch Factory on Yale Boulevard and Ash.

Carl D. Franke, Sr., saw the industry blossom. Paris Cleaning Company filled the three-story building, and six delivery trucks and two motorcycles criss-crossed the city regularly.

Paris has always used petroleum-based Stoddart solvent. This cleaner is recognized for its safety, its gentle and high-quality cleaning, and its minimal odor. Because of the petroleum base, however, the solvent was affected by fuel rationing during World War II. Forced to close, Paris sold the building to the John W. Hobbs Corporation.

The third generation, Carl D. Franke, Jr., reopened the business after World War II at its present location, 1013 East Ash, in a new plant designed especially for dry cleaning. The business became Paris Cleaners and Furriers and included a certified, cold-below-freezing fur vault and two garment storage vaults. A shirt laundry was added in the early 1960s, and five branch pick-up locations were built throughout the community.

Bette H. Franke became president in 1981. Expansion into wedding gown and period gown restoration, and suede, leather, upholstery, and rug cleaning met the community's growing needs and was

reflected in the company's new name, Paris Fabricare Specialists, Inc.

A fourth generation of the Franke family now manages the company. Glenda Franke McNichols is president and F. Sheplor Franke is executive vice president; C. David Franke III has also served as president.

Environmental and social issues are two ongoing business concerns. Continued use of the Stoddart solvent protects the environment. Paris is involved in a recycling program for plastic garment bags and hangers. In addition the company collects used clothes for groups that distribute to the needy at no charge.

Dry cleaning is a craft made more challenging by the introduction of man-made fibers. In order to meet these needs, Paris management continually learns new techniques. Carl Franke, Jr., is a past president of the Illinois State Fabricare Association. He, C. David Franke III, and F. Sheplor Franke are Springfield's only alumni of the International Fabricare Institute. Active association involvement and course completions by all members of the Paris leadership team assure customers that each garment is cleaned thoroughly, prepared professionally, and returned with pride.

The third and fourth generations of the Franke family now own and manage Paris Fabricare. They are, seated, Glenda Franke McNichols; standing, from left, C. David Franke III, Bette H. Franke, Carl D. Franke, Jr., and F. Sheplor Franke.

CDS Office Systems

"Customers First" is more than a slogan at CDS Office Systems—it is the overriding philosophy and way of life for this more than 20-year-old firm. Founded by Jerome L. Watson in 1972, CDS Office Systems is now the largest office-machine service company in central Illinois. With offices in Champaign, Bloomington, Peoria, and Macomb, as well as its headquarters in Springfield, CDS offers a complete line of modern office equipment, products, and supplies.

Beginning as Copier Duplicating Specialists, CDS quickly expanded from duplicating into also selling copying equipment. From its first line of Saxton copiers, CDS added Minolta, and others soon followed. Computers, printers, and facsimile machines were added. Eventually, printing, as well as duplicating services were provided with the formation of ColorWorld, the color printing division of CDS. Today, the complete line of state-of-the-art office equipment includes Minolta (for more than 18 years), Panasonic, and Konica.

As its customers' technological needs grew rapidly, so did CDS. From a beginning staff of three to more than 100 today, and from a single building to the entire block, CDS maintains its leadership in a rapidly changing, increasingly high-tech competitive industry.

Innovation, technology, service, and people support its customer-first philosophy. Innovation in products and services keeps CDS on the leading edge of the office-equipment industry. Providing a continuous array of top-quality, technologically-advanced products ensures that CDS can meet and exceed its customers' changing needs. Exemplary service, the foundation of CDS' success, guarantees that the expertise is readily available to keep customers' businesses running effectively and efficiently. And finally, well-trained and highly motivated people, the backbone of the company, earn CDS its reputation as a value-added, customer-focused company.

Building long-term, working relationships with its suppliers as well as its customers is also an essential tenet of the operating philosophy of CDS Office Systems. Representing more than 250 manufacturers, CDS has established itself as a comprehensive source for office equipment and supplies throughout central Illinois.

The future looks bright for CDS. From optical disc-drive storage, the wave of the future for filing, to systems for identifying problems, to multi-function products for small businesses, CDS maintains its dedication to meeting the needs of its central Illinois customers. As an innovative dealer in the office equipment industry, CDS is committed to staying close to its customers, continually assessing their needs, and developing cost-effective solutions.

Maldaner's

Maldaner's has changed locations, expanded its services, and consistently diversified its menu, but it has been a Springfield name synonymous with good food since 1884.

Its current Sixth Street building, constructed in 1894, was actually founder John Maldaner's third downtown site. This son of a Milwaukee mattress maker began as a caterer and baker, eventually expanding with a soda fountain and sit-down dining. Reprinted old photos, art deco wall stencils, and a pressed-tin ceiling are vivid reminders of this restaurant's history.

Carolyn and Robert Oxtoby are the current owners of both the building and the restaurant. Buying the building in the 1960s, Carolyn saw that it reflected a trend of building neglect and underuse in downtown Springfield. During the next decade, she plunged ahead and remodeled the second floor into a second restaurant and the third floor into apartments. Since the mechanical systems did not meet city building codes, the task was monumental. These efforts reflected her philosophy of maintaining existing downtown

buildings and expanding their functions.

Oxtoby eventually assumed ownership of both the downstairs restaurant, which had existed for decades, and the newly opened upstairs gourmet restaurant. Although the menus are distinctly different for each restaurant, a tradition of excellent service and delicious food are trademarks of each.

Maldaner's Upstairs is a gourmet restaurant. Except for Beef Wellington, served since the restaurant opened in 1977, the menu changes frequently. Wild game, new treatments of standard main dishes, and interesting appetizers highlight the menu. Also known for a wide assortment of excellent foods, the street-level restaurant features a completely different menu.

A visit with restaurant manager and chef Michael Higgins and his wife, Nancy, amid a cornucopia of delightful aromas, explains some of the restaurant's successes. For instance, they carefully plan seasonal appetizers, grow all the restaurant's herbs. and use fresh foods in their from-scratch recipes. New recipes are apt to come from Higgins' kitchen creations, as well as from other restaurants or gourmet magazines.

Maldaner's is also reintroducing its catering services. Appropriately, today's catered events are often hosted by grandchildren of those Springfield families who enjoyed the delicacies once prepared by John Maldaner.

Embarking on their second century, both the building and the restaurant have witnessed and been part of a changing Springfield scene. What has remained constant is the reputation for a quality dining experience at Maldaner's.

....
Below Left:
Maldaner's manager and chef Michael Higgins and owner Carolyn Oxtoby pose in front of the landmark Springfield restaurant.
Above:
Rehabilitation of the 1894 building's second floor created a separate gourmet restaurant, bar, and individual areas for receptions, parties, and banquets. The work reflects a philosophy of expanding the use of downtown buildings.
....

Watts Copy Systems, Inc.

I f the concept of excellence in service had not already been a key to business success, Watts Copy Systems, Inc., probably would have invented it. The products, people, philosophy, and actions of the central Illinois firm support its motto, "Where service is more than a promise."

Sharp copiers and facsimiles and Hasler postage equipment are the only brands stocked by Watts Copy Systems. "By specializing in only one manufacturer, Sharp, we are able to dedicate our resources to maintaining adequate supply and parts inventories which are critical to the proper maintenance of our products," explains Carol Watts. In 1984 a separate division was created to provide an alternative to Pitney Bowes. ASCOM/Hasler postage equipment is the choice of eight out of 10 mail rooms, Carol points out.

Watts Copy Systems employs approximately 90 people in seven locations, offering complete

sales and service throughout central and southern Illinois. Each employee's commitment to service and customer satisfaction is a continuing goal. Personal pride and accomplishment are reflected in each employee, the cornerstone of the company's success.

At the heart of the customer-oriented products and people is a philosophy of caring. Five company service dispatchers coordinate the firm's same-day service. From their dispatch centers, Watts' service staff consistently responds to service calls in four hours or less— one of the fastest responses in the industry today.

The company also employs a factory-certified trainer who conducts Sharp service schools at the new 17,500-square-foot headquarters. Watts is one of only a few dealerships making this commitment to training.

Does this dedication to service produce results? Absolutely! Less than two years after opening for business, Watts Copy Systems earned the prestigious Hyakuman-Kai Award from Sharp for purchases of more than one million dollars. In 1991 they received the Elite Hyakuman Kai Award, one of only 37 dealers in the United States. Nationwide industry figures show that Watts recently installed more copiers than any other dealer in this market area. Overall satisfaction is supported by a 98 percent customer-retention rate.

The company is also deeply committed to the cities in which it is located. "We feel strongly that we should give a portion back to the communities which have supported our company," Skip Watts explains.

For instance Watts Copy Systems contributes to a Carle Clinic golf outing in Champaign, a secretaries' party in Decatur, and an Oktoberfest in Quincy. In Springfield the firm has supported such diverse community activities as ballets, Rail Charity Classic, Festival of Trees, and Crimestoppers.

George Alarm

Computerized, specialized, and highly personalized—George Alarm Company has led the security industry in central Illinois for 36 years.

Donald and Jeannette George established George Alarm Company in 1957 during the infancy of the security industry. The company has always been at the forefront of the burgeoning industry and Donald and Jeannette were the driving force behind it in central Illinois. Since its inception the staff at George Alarm Company has lived by the motto "Dedicated to Protecting You."

Living up to this bold motto, in 1983 the company constructed the first Underwriters Laboratory approved central monitoring station in Springfield. Underwriters Laboratory (U.L.) imposed strict requirements for construction of the central station to ensure operation during disaster or attack. The central station contains state of the art computers with direct hot lines to all emergency services. Since dialing is not required, operators can report alarm signals almost instantaneously. The central station includes completely redundant systems and its own electrical generator to ensure operation 24 hours a day, every day.

Building a U.L. approved central station is only one of many firsts. George Alarm Company commits itself to providing their customers with

the best security service possible. Providing the best service possible requires a willingness to invest in the most advanced equipment. George Alarm Company invested in the first U.L. approved radio monitoring network in central Illinois and pioneered its use for various advanced security applications. The radio monitoring network is completely independent from the phone system and therefore not subject to phone system failures. The company made a second aggressive investment by installing a U.L. approved two-way radio monitoring system. The central station now ranks as one of the most advanced in the country. Two-way radio, still exclusive to George Alarm Company in central Illinois, represents the ultimate in high security protection and is the most secure method of alarm monitoring available today. The company continues to lead the industry operating the largest locally owned security company in central Illinois, with offices in Springfield, Decatur, Champaign, and Bloomington.

Peers in the industry saw George Alarm Company's drive for perfection and quality and invited the company to join the exclusive Central Station Alarm Asociation (CSAA). CSAA, a national organization, invites for membership only those companies showing excellence in central station quality and operation. George Alarm Company is the city's only company approved for membership.

From modest beginnings as a family-owned business operated from a garage, to one of the country's top 100 security companies, as printed in Security Distributing and Marketing 1991 and 1992, George Alarm Company is poised for high-tech changes in the future. A constant throughout the company's existence has been the dedication to remain on the leading edge of the security idustry. Security is George Alarm Company's only business and they are proud to be the best.

Above:
Donald J. George, founder of
George Alarm Company.
Left:
George Alarm Company
headquarters in
Springfield, Illinois.

Southern Illinois University School of Medicine

Southern Illinois University School of Medicine is more than a training ground for future physicians. It is a sophisticated medical research facility and a source for many direct medical services unavailable elsewhere in Illinois, outside of Chicago.

SIU School of Medicine was founded in 1970, following a call for a downstate medical school to train physicians and help Illinois meet its health care needs. Since SIU's first class of 24 graduated in 1975, over 1,100 men and women have received medical degrees, and more than 700 residents and fellows have completed postgraduate specialty training. In keeping with the school's original mission, more than 40 percent of the medical- student alumni and nearly half the resident alumni now practice in Illinois.

The school's mission continues today in three complementary areas:
- Programs in undergraduate, graduate, and continuing medical education;
- Direct primary- and specialty-care medical services to patients; and
- Research into basic medical and clinical sciences.

Medical schools from around the world continue to study SIU's innovative, competency-based curriculum. Here, medical students receive considerable hands-on training and firsthand experience in diagnostic techniques, including the use of real and simulated patients. Other courses, including medical humanities, ensure that students complement their clinical expertise with human compassion.

While the school's original intent—training physicians for Illinois—remains firmly in place, its overall mission has broadened to include greater emphasis on research and the clinical practice of medicine. More than 110 full-time physicians on SIU's faculty perform three roles—teachers, practicing physicians, and researchers. Therefore SIU physicians not only provide care today as practicing physicians, they touch the future through their training of new physicians, and help advance medicine through clinical and laboratory research. Much of their care of patients in Springfield occurs in two affiliated hospitals, Memorial Medical Center and St. John's Hospital.

There are more than 235,000 patient visits to SIU Physicians and Surgeons annually for diagnosis and treatment. Primary care is provided by faculty in family practice, internal medicine, obstetrics and gynecology, and pediatrics. In addition, SIU Physicians and Surgeons offer many specialty services not available elsewhere in downstate Illinois:
- Neuroscience specialties are provided through the Center for Alzheimer's Disease and Related Disorders, and the Center for Epilepsy.
- Plastic and reconstructive surgery services include a Midwest center for microsurgery and replantation, burn care, a skin culture laboratory, hyperbaric oxygen therapy, and hand therapy.
- Women's health services include cancer treatment by gynecologic oncologists.
- A kidney transplant program operates in conjunction with Memorial Medical Center.
- The SIU Eye Center treats corneal diseases, glaucoma, low vision, retinal and vitreous conditions, and pediatric eye disorders.

Below:

The School of Medicine's physician specialists include plastic and reconstructive surgeons who have developed a Midwest center for microsurgery and replantation.

- The Motion Analysis Laboratory provides unique diagnostic and treatment plans for patients with gait abnormalities, and an orthotics and prosthetics program which includes the computer-aided manufacture of artificial limbs.

At any given time more than 150 projects are under way in SIU School of Medicine's clinical and laboratory research programs. More than $10 million in grants annually supports efforts such as:

- SIU's nationally recognized auditory research team that studies hearing loss and how the brain processes sound;
- Research on spinal cord injury treatment and prevention by specialists in orthopaedics and rehabilitation;
- Cardiovascular care research to investigate hypertension, coronary diseases, strokes, and the development of new drugs;
- Alzheimer's disease research including development of a diagnostic test for the disease and studies on drugs that may improve patients' cognitive abilities;
- Plastic and reconstructive surgery projects including studying skin culture techniques, microsurgical advancements, and applications of hyperbaric medicine;
- Numerous clinical trials of new drugs which make state-of-the-art treatments available locally before they are released nationwide.

The increase of clinical services and research has prompted several additions to SIU's physical plant. The Medical Instructional Facility on North Rutledge, completed in 1977, includes lecture halls, a teaching museum, a medical library of

some 130,000 volumes, the Professional Development Laboratory teaching facility, and research laboratories. The Springfield Combined Laboratory Facility, completed in 1988, houses laboratories and offices for the School of Medicine, the Illinois Department of Public Health, and the Illinois Environmental Protection Agency.

With the completion in 1988 of the five-story Pavilion at St. John's Hospital, many of the school's examination and procedure rooms, support services, and offices were relocated for easier patient access. Opened in 1993, the SIU Clinics, a joint project of the School of Medicine and Memorial Medical Center, will consolidate several SIU outpatient clinics under one roof. A new SIU Plastic and Reconstructive Surgery Institute will be located in an adjoining building.

Greater Springfield has felt a strong economic impact as a result of having the SIU School of Medicine based here. With a local work force of more than 1,000, the school contributes about $85.5 million annually in direct spending to Sangamon County. Using standard Department of Labor multipliers, an estimated $327 million in purchasing power is created as that money recycles through the Illinois economy. About 40 percent of SIU's income is derived from state funding; the remainder comes from such sources as research grants, clinic income, and gifts.

Southern Illinois University School of Medicine contributes a great deal to the quality of life enjoyed by the people of Greater Springfield—more than can be measured in dollars, and perhaps more than any amount of money could buy.

Left:
The school's administrative center, a four-story building at 801 N. Rutledge, includes classrooms, laboratories, offices, a medical museum, and a library.
Below:
The innovative curriculum at SIU School of Medicine includes considerable training experience for medical students in diagnostic techniques, including the use of real and simulated patients.

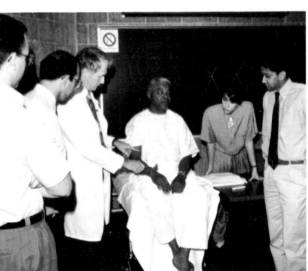

Memorial Medical Center

Memorial Medical Center's commitment to meeting patient needs is demonstrated throughout the teaching environment of this full-service community hospital.

Late in May 1991 Memorial dedicated a $23-million addition. This 125,000-square-foot structure includes the Regional Cancer Center, 16 surgery suites, a 38-bed medical patient unit, and a new main lobby and admitting area.

The Regional Cancer Center now combines medical oncology and radiation oncology in the same building with physician offices, clinical areas, and treatment rooms. Centralizing patient services results in more convenient scheduling and more rapid treatment. An integral part of the Regional Cancer Center is research conducted in conjunction with the National Cancer Institute and with private pharmaceutical and biotechnology companies.

The new surgical suites increase Memorial's total number of operating rooms to 20. Each new suite will accommodate lasers and other state-of-the-art technologies. Two suites also offer fluoroscopy equipment for urology procedures. Two others have laminar flow units for total joint replacement.

Soon after the dedication, Memorial took part in a ground-breaking for two new structures to be built in conjunction with Southern Illinois University School of Medicine and private developers. A wide variety of outpatient clinical and surgical programs will be housed in these new structures.

Much more than buildings and equipment, however, people are at the heart of Memorial Medical Center—patients with unique needs, dedicated physi-

cians, staff with specialized training to meet those needs, and volunteers with talents to help patients and support the staff. The Regional Kidney Center, the Regional Burn Center, Comprehensive Cardiology Services, a designated Trauma Center, Neuromuscular Sciences, Psychiatry, the Eye Center—all contribute to Memorial's standing as a regional health care leader.

Nonmedical services include Memorial's Gold Club, which meets the needs of all people eligible for Medicare. Memorial Child Care opened in response to employee's needs for a flexible child-care program.

Projects of the Memorial Medical Center Foundation, Friends of Memorial, Memorial Medical Center Auxiliary, and Memorial's Volunteer Program vary widely. They include funding colon cancer screening programs, making items for patient use, staffing the hospital gift shop, and organizing seminars on health-related issues.

Memorial has grown immensely since it began in 1897 as a 12-bed hospital in a doctor's home on the corner of Fifth and North Grand. It will continue to grow in the future to meet the health and wellness needs of central and southern Illinois residents.

The face of Memorial Medical Center changed when a $23-million, 125,000-square-foot addition opened in 1991. The Regional Cancer Center, more surgery suites, and a medical patient unit are part of this expansion.

St. John's Hospital

The history of St. John's Hospital dates back to 1875 when Hospital Sisters of the Third Order of St. Francis journeyed from Germany to Springfield to carry out their healing mission. Today, with more than 750 beds, St. John's is the largest hospital in Springfield and one of the largest Catholic hospitals in the United States.

The sisters brought with them dedication and commitment to caring for the sick and injured. They were pioneers in hospital care for people throughout the Sangamon River Valley. Currently, through Hospital Sisters Health System, the sisters operate 13 hospitals in Illinois and Wisconsin.

The growth of St. John's Hospital parallels the community's increasingly complex healthcare needs. The first permanent hospital building was opened in 1879 and housed 16 patients. By 1902, 80 sisters were engaged in or studying nursing in the hospital, which could then house 150 patients. The current 12-story building, which replaced the original building, was built in 1939.

In 1967 a $40-million expansion project and modernization program began. This new complex of buildings was completed in 1975. In 1977 St. John's-North, a center for transitional care, rehabilitation, adult day care, hospice, and Libertas chemical dependency treatment program, was added. St. John's Hospice, a program for terminally ill patients, is the first in Springfield.

The first open-heart surgery in Springfield was performed at St. John's in 1964. Today St. John's Heart Center provides extensive cardiac services ranging from diagnostic to rehabilitative. The hospital pioneered the use of thrombolytic agents for immediate treatment of heart attack. More than 1,000 open-heart surgeries are performed at the center each year.

St. John's is a regional health care center. More than 45 percent of its patients come from outside Sangamon County. The hospital employs over 3,200 people, making it the second-largest employer in the Springfield area. More than 540

physicians and dentists are on the medical staff.

The hospital also serves as a regional Trauma/Emergency Medical Services Center, Poison Resource Center, High Risk Neonatal Center, and a high-risk maternity referral center. The High Risk Neonatal Center (HRNC) celebrated its 50th anniversary of service in 1991. The HRNC serves a 33-county area in central Illinois. Originally the center's focus was to help low birth-weight babies. Now the center provides care for infants with a wide range of medical and surgical needs as well.

St. John's has the only pediatric intensive-care unit in downstate Illinois. The unit is available for critically ill patients from infancy through age 18.

St. John's Pavilion, an ambulatory service center and medical office building, opened in 1988. Pavilion services include day surgery, cardiovascular diagnostics, the Cancer Institute, and gastroenterology. The Pavilion also houses Southern Illinois University School of Medicine clinics and faculty.

As St. John's Hospital moves into the future, the institution remains committed to the Hospital Sisters' philosophy of the intrinsic value and dignity of human life. Through constant dedication to that philosophy, St. John's continues to provide the finest healthcare services available.

**Below:
St. John's serves as a regional
Trauma/Emergency Medical
Services Center.**

Robert Morris College

Robert Morris College students are told to think of their first day at the private college as their first day at a new job. Whether they are recent high school graduates or adults returning to school, all are expected to live up to the four A's: Academics, Appearance, Attendance, and Attitude.

Robert Morris College (RMC) is accredited by the North Central Association of Colleges and Schools. With school vacations limited to occasional days, rather than weeks, students may earn either a diploma in 10 months or an associate degree in 15 months. To earn a diploma, students take courses which are concentrated in their career path. Students earning their associate degree also broaden their education in the areas of communications, humanities, math and science, and social and behavioral sciences.

Just as on the job, appearance and class attendance are important for RMC students. They are expected to dress as they would in the work place, and report in if they are unable to attend class. Beyond their commitment to studies, student attitudes include a willingness to demonstrate extended professionalism through community involvement. Community services such as food

baskets, a seasonal angel tree, and fund-raising events are an integral part of student life.

RMC supports the four A's with a personalized atmosphere and integration of coursework standards with work-world expectations. Each student meets regularly with his or her program director to review academic successes, plan career paths, and discuss possible problems, even if those difficulties are not school related. With its "Career Strategies" and "College Prep" programs, RMC helps both traditional and the nontraditional students build confidence in their skills to ensure college success. RMC's lifetime job placement program for graduates is supplemented by an ongoing career development program. Success of the career placement program is demonstrated by a 97-percent average job-placement rate within 15 weeks of graduation.

The Springfield campus opened in July 1988, but the college traces its roots back to 1913 with the founding of Chicago's Moser School, an outstanding independent business institution. RMC was chartered in 1965 and offered associate degrees in both vocational and liberal arts programs at the school's Carthage campus. In 1975 the college acquired the Moser School.

The college is named after a man who represented both the colonial Commonwealth of Pennsylvania as a signer of the Declaration of Independence and the Constitution of the United States. He has been called "The Financier of the Revolution." Robert Morris Collge is proud to continue that tradition of success through a caring philosophy and a quality education.

Right:
The Springfield campus of Robert Morris College opened in 1988. Students elect to earn either a diploma or an associate's degree from the college.
Below:
Traditional and nontraditional students work with the staff at Robert Morris College to build confidence in their individual skills and to ensure college success.

Partners in Excellence Index

GREATER SPRINGFIELD
Building on the Legacy

By Michael P. Murphy, Edward J. Russo,
Pam Bruzan, Sharon Zara

Photographs by Terry Farmer

Historical photographs courtesy, Sangamon Valley Collection, Lincoln Library

Edited by Christopher Phillips, Nancy Jackson

Senior Editor, Jeffrey Reeves

Designed by Jonathan Wieder

Photo Editor, Robin L. Sterling

Managing Editor: Linda J. Hreno. *Coordinator:* Kelly Goulding. *Proofreaders:* Martha Cheresh, Lin Schonberger. *Editorial Assistant:* Kimberly J. Pelletier. *Assistant Coordinator:* Erin Goulding.

Production Manager: Jeffrey Scott Hayes. *Art Production:* Amanda Howard. *Manager, Computer Systems:* Steve Zehngut.

Printed in the United States of America, 1993. All rights reserved, including the right of reproduction in whole or in part in any form. J. Kelley Younger, *Publisher and Editor-in-Chief.* Terry Pender, *Controller.*

Produced by CCA Publications, Inc., 22323-6 Sherman Way, P.O. Box 267, West Hills, CA 91303, (818) 710-1627. Nellie Scott, *President.*